BELIEVING IN ME

STORIES ABOUT SURVIVAL—
BEATING THE ODDS IN FLIGHT AND IN ACADEMIA

DONALD V. HUARD, PH.D.

Professor of Psychology - Emeritus

Maricopa County Community College District
(Arizona)

authorHOUSE®

AuthorHouse™
1663 Liberty Drive
Bloomington, IN 47403
www.authorhouse.com
Phone: 833-262-8899

Published by AuthorHouse 10/04/2022

ISBN: 978-1-7283-0078-8 (sc)
ISBN: 978-1-7283-0077-1 (e)

Library of Congress Control Number: 2019901956

CONTENTS

INTRODUCTION

When I was a young man in my early thirties, sharing the burdens of raising four pre-teen children with my wife Marie, I so often thought about how old I would be one distant day when mankind entered the new millennium. I had it figured out that I would be sixty-seven years old when the twenty-first century began. Then, the millennium was many years away. As the year 2000 arrived I would be a retired citizen with nearly forty years of experience as a husband, parent and an educational psychologist. That was way off in the distant future, when I would be old and grey.

What I didn't know when our children were young was that the next thirty years would go by as though they took only a single decade. It's astounding to discover that you have become an older person well before you had planned it. Teaching in the classroom month after month, year after year while watching our pre-teens become teenagers, then young adults, then full grown mature adults with their own little children made us focus on them rather than ourselves. Oblivious to time, I became an old grey-haired grandpa before I realized what was happening.

How was I to know when I was thirty that my first marriage would end just after I turned fifty? How was I to know that the loss of Marie to illness in 1981 would be followed by what I have since referred to as a "super, second" life? How could I have imagined during the pain of the loss of my children's mom that a new life was to follow, one that is also filled with love and devotion, a marriage of great good fortune for me that, in its thirty-sixth year continues to grow in strength and commitment?

I fought several major battles during my lifetime, battles that took courage to fight, courage that I didn't know I had. The first was at the age of nineteen when I was to become a well trained combat infantryman in the United States Army. I was at a very significant disadvantage having been drafted during the Korean conflict in 1952 just after I had suffered from a quite severe illness that brought my weight down to only 115 lbs!

The story of my struggle to survive the rigors of basic training and my subsequent assignment as a fixed-wing aircraft mechanic will take several chapters to tell. It was a stressful time, yet an exciting time during which I experienced troop ship travel in the Bering sea west of Russia and two tours of duty on an airstrip in a remote village in central Alaska. In Galena, I served with the 30th Engineers Base Topological Brigade, a unit designated the job of surveying the vast land of what would become the 49th American state in 1959. It was a dangerous assignment for which I was paid extra "hazardous duty" pay for risking my life a number of times flying over the treacherous Alaskan terrain.

The second major career oriented struggle took place long after my release from the military and after nearly twenty years of academic training that resulted in my long teaching career at Phoenix Community College. Having earned an associate in arts degree, a bachelor's degree and a master's degree as a psychology major, I needed only the support of a committee of professors as I wrote my doctoral dissertation to complete my program and get my Ph.D. degree. My candidacy, however, was challenged by the chairman of the psychology department who set up what I felt were unreasonable additional requirements before he was willing to encourage my progress. I resisted those requirements and as a result, I was viewed by the chairman as an uncooperative candidate in need of additional coursework and a repeat of my comprehensive examination before he would even set up a dissertation committee.

On the advice of another faculty member, I decided to appeal the chairman's requirements before the dean of the College of Liberal Arts, a move that was further resented by that chairman. He added yet more requirements leaving me with the impression that I would never be able to get my Ph.D. degree!

What followed was a two and a half year struggle on my part to get support at the University administration level for the elimination of the additional requirements. I was forced to decide if I should give up a twenty year dream of becoming a doctor of psychology or if I should fight for a more direct route to the successful completion of my program. Feeling that I was being treated unfairly and in spite of my reluctance to take on the system, I decided to fight!

I have never been a man of courage, but I just could not let my dream end in failure because of the excessive demands of a mean-spirited chairman of the psychology department who fought relentlessly to prevent me from getting my degree. It became obvious to me that he did resent my attempt to override his requirements and that he would likely see to it that I would fail in any subsequent repeat of a comprehensive examination. Requiring a candidate who had passed those exams once to repeat them was an unheard of requirement (not applied to my knowledge, to any other candidate) that should not have been arbitrarily applied in my case.

The story of my battle for a just solution to be decided in my favor took me up through the hierarchy of the University including the office of the vice president! It's a very long story that takes up three chapters in this book. As the reader who patiently goes through the story in all of its detail will see, I did win out in the end. With the eventual help of a number of professors and a very understanding gentleman from the college of law, I did prevail.

But my long sought-after achievement left me with some definite long term emotional scars. My review of the conflict will reveal how the fight affected my self-image and even had a serious effect on my marriage. I faced up to the frustration and humiliation to which I was unjustly subjected, but the battle was quite costly for my family. Was it worth the fight? My patient readers will have to decide...

But, enough on the difficulties in the military and at the University (for now) that seem to be such negative concerns. It is my intention to write my insignificant little story as a positive reflection of the wonderful things that have happened to me throughout my lifetime with a little less emphasis on the sad parts and a greater emphasis on the good things that have made my life worthwhile and ultimately quite fulfilling.

The wonderful feelings of a life well-lived, children well-raised, career objectives attained and contributions to others in the classroom serve as sufficient rewards for the prices paid. Many times, throughout my later years, I have thought about the responsibility I have to convey a positive mental outlook about life to my children. Life is too short to be lived unhappily or experienced as a cross to bear, shrouded in self-sacrificing servitude. Life is to be lived joyously, the early years to be lived with some willing enthusiasm for challenge. The mature years should be rich with contentment and the power of positive reflection.

On the pages that follow, you will find my expressions of gratitude to the people who influenced me in a positive way, to those who raised me, those who pushed me along, those who helped me pick myself up when clobbered by life and those who assured me that they appreciated my efforts.

For what they are worth, I'll include a few reflections about life that have taken over ninety years to develop, years that went by so quickly that the millennium arrived over twenty years ago. One thing is sure, the attitudes I held when I was just a boy of twenty changed significantly through my thirties, forties and fifties, so much so that I am clearly not the same person today. The old man is more than just the youth plus the passage of time.

The major motivation for this book, however, is to be found in my determination to effectively communicate much about my life to my children and my grandchildren. Maybe my own children will come to recognize and accept the fact that when I was a young parent to them and a bit less attendant to their special needs and interests, I was fighting some of my own demons and dragons.

I hope as they read this book, they will find reason to be proud of me, as I am of them. I hope they will be proud of grandpa for his fighting spirit. I hope they will understand and be forgiving toward him in spite of his preoccupations. Above all, I hope they will be loving toward him during his declining years.

CHAPTER ONE

THE FIGHTING MACHINE - 1952

Imagine my delight when I discovered that the mailbox contained a letter for me that bore the official seal of the President of the United States of America!

October 26, 1952

Dear Mr. Donald Huard,

Greetings from the office of the President: You have been selected by a committee of your local peers to serve in the armed services of the United States of America. You will be expected to appear at 201 N First Avenue, Phoenix, Arizona at 7:00 A. M on November 28, 1952 for induction into the United States Army.

Sincerely yours,
Dwight David Eisenhower
President of the United States

"I like Ike - I like Ike!" That's what the voters cheered at the political convention for the republicans in late 1951. The election that followed showed that a great many voters agreed with the slogan, enough to elect the former military general and hero overwhelmingly over Adlai Stevenson, the popular governor of the state of Illinois. As Eisenhower's predecessor, Harry Truman had lost much of his popularity as the democratic president during the latter part of his term because of his firm decision to support the South Koreans against invasion from the north across the 38th parallel in the Korean Peninsula.

Later in the conflict, Truman fired the popular General Douglas McArthur who wanted to invade the north, and also China to punish the communists for their transgressions. This had further eroded Truman's presidential popularity. Eisenhower, on the other hand, had few popularity problems, that is, except with young Donald Huard who didn't particularly care for his mailing habits.

I had just turned eighteen in May of that year, was working for a kindly, considerate boss at the Maytag store and was recovering from a very severe case of what at that time was called the "Asian" flu. My boss sent me home for a few days to heave and weave. That became three weeks of self-pity and weight loss.

When I "checked in" for active military duty a few weeks later I looked like I had just been released from a WW II prison camp. I weighed only 115 lbs!

Dad took me down to the recruiting station that unhappy morning for my induction. On the way there, he told me not to let my mind get too far away from home and those who loved me. My dear dad could be surprisingly sentimental at times. I do remember, when I was inside the building after we said goodbye, I looked out through the window and saw him with his forehead leaning sadly downward against the top of the Chevy steering wheel. His two other sons had survived the big war. And then came the Korean conflict. We both wondered what was ahead. For me, it was a long bus ride to Fort Ord in California near San Francisco.

From that 07:00 A.M. on November 28, 1952 until 02:00 P.M. on November 27, 1954 I maintained a most remarkable hate relationship with anything and everything military. I looked like Ichabod Crane in my too-big uniform. They yanked my two front teeth. Everyone else was twice as strong as I was and (I thought) half as scared as I was. Nobody was more homesick than I was.

There I was, fifty pounds lighter than the others, so skinny that I could hide behind my rifle, trying to act like a big tough dude, a real mean fighting machine... I'm sure any North Korean soldier confronted by me would have been terrified.

As you might guess, they don't have a lot of patience with frail mamma's boys when you are in basic training. So I got yelled at more than most of the others, picked on more than the others and did more K P duty than most of the others. However, I did the best that I could and it apparently worked as I did survive. I learned to clown a bit. If any 200 pounder got on my tail and gave me any lip I would loudly tell him I was gonna kick his ass and I would dance around him jabbing at the air while every one laughed. My own left hook was so vicious it nearly knocked *me* off my feet. Whew! Survived another one...

Surprisingly, especially to myself, I soon began to toughen up. After about three weeks or so I began to think that I might actually get through basic training alive! The calisthenics were grueling. That M-1 rifle was a lot heavier for me than it was for the other guys. They should have trained me on a BB gun. It seemed as though we ran all day long. We ran to chow, to the rifle range, to the infiltration course, to the latrine. I wondered at that time why the army needed so many trucks. They sure didn't seem to use them. I never knew my feet could hurt so much.

On the rifle range I did quite well. I fired sharpshooter with the M-1 rifle. Nine rounds then "Ping," out would fly the empty clip. Stuff another one in while keeping your thumb clear and fire away again. Each raw recruit got his thumb caught in the breech of that weapon only once. It was a lesson learned quickly and completely with only one trial. I did better with the M-1 carbine, a .30 caliber rifle often used for closer combat. It was much lighter. I could handle it better and I actually got an X-pert marksmanship medal for my performance. Then there was the heavier Browning automatic rifle (BAR) that could be "fanned" to fire only a single round in order to fool the enemy into thinking that it was only an M-1 rifle. Then we went to mortars and learned how to drop round after round into a thirty foot radius using a method called bracketing.

During the first days of basic training, the recruit's world becomes one of disorientation, confusion and pain. It was never like this at home. Mom used to wake me up in the mid-morning by gently calling me or nudging my lazy bones. At Fort Ord the cadre walked into the barracks at 04;00 A.M. and dropped a grenade simulator into an empty garbage can. I went from prone to panic in a nanosecond.

Fighting on the bayonet course, firing on the rifle ranges and running the rest of each day left us all exhausted by 11:00 P. M. bedtime. I would lay in the dark listening to the snoring of others that sounded like mine does today, trying not to go to sleep because I knew that grenade would go off, giving new meaning to the Big Bang theory. As a survival mechanism I developed a little technique. I would lay on my back thinking about the events of the day, trying to process my head until I felt a little more in contact with reality, then flip over onto my stomach and enjoy five hours of blissful splendor before Sergeant Macho came in to "gently" awaken me. The lasting effect of this is that even now I can't go to sleep on my back. If I stay on my back I will stay awake. Since I am old now, however, when I just flip to my stomach I will still lay awake.

A buddy of mine had another trick that helped him deal with the discomforts and miseries of military life. He talked the fellows at the supply window into issuing him combat boots that were two sizes too small. On the rifle range and on the long marches he would groan and agonize over the condition of his feet. Yet, he still wore those boots every day. We tried telling him to get bigger boots. "Look," he would say, "I got drafted and here I am. The sergeant is on my ass all of the time. I keep busting my thumb in that damn rifle. My dog back home got killed by a bus. My wife is divorcing me. The only time I feel good is when I take off these effin' boots!"

All of the recruits were gathered onto a very large set of bleachers one day to witness a demonstration of the firing of a most remarkable weapon. Called a recoilless rifle, this 57 millimeter "canon" was resting on a tripod about twenty yards in front of us. That artillery piece was amazingly powerful for something small enough to be fired from the shoulder. The cadre (usually the high ranking corporals) gave us a memorable demonstration. The back breech of the weapon is open, resulting in the back blast that counters the muzzle pressure that propels a high explosive anti-tank shell that can be accurately placed on a target 2,000 yards distant! When the gun goes off, there is no recoil whatever. Because of the open breech the sound of that thing going off is very deafening.

When it was time for a raw, dumb recruit to fire it, guess who got picked from the crowd? On rubbery knees, I got next to that thing and waited just as instructed until corporal Bravo loaded the charge. "Just like with the M-1, take a deep breath, sight in that old tank out there, exhale slowly with your mouth open and squeeze the trigger," I was told. Well, there's always that ten percent that don't get the word. I forgot the open the mouth part. When that damned thing went off I thought the charge had hit my head. It was like a 747 jet with a flaming afterburner was flying in my right inner ear. I turned to the corporal I couldn't hear and saw him shaking his fist at me as he kicked at me, chasing me back into the bleachers. Apparently, the safest place to be was in the tank I was shooting at. I missed the target by over fifty yards! The reason you keep your mouth open is because some of the air pressure can enter the throat and the eustachian tubes to the middle ears to counter the pressure on the outer eardrums when the blast occurs. I didn't. And it didn't. So I sustained a broken eardrum!

I worked amidst the jet airplanes doing KP duty in the chow hall the next day and I couldn't hear the metal trays crashing against the metal counter tops. Those were the days when a broken eardrum meant you got aspirin from the old infirmary and were sent back to your unit to heal on your own. Now, the recruit would get a medical discharge, go on disability and be supported by Uncle Sam forever. I went on for a few more days of policing the kitchen in high pitched ecstasy before returning to my regular duties on the infiltration course. My hearing is still a bit weak on the right side. Happily, that's the side my wife is on when I'm driving.

The Korean police action raged on as my two months of basic training progressed. Tests were given to determine if we were good candidates for special schools like the officer candidate school, clerk typist school, dental technician school or paramedic school, etc. I flunked them all. Any fellow who had bombed his way through high school, as I had was learning deficient, a poor prospect for anything other than two more months of infantry training. So I was to climb taller hills, carried bigger weapons, crawled longer infiltration courses under "enemy" gunfire and learned how to dig in to escape from a barrage of incoming artillery. As my training neared its end I began to resign myself to the idea that I would be sent to Korea as a foot soldier to apply my new skills, none of which I had ever asked for and all of which I despised.

Then came one of the proudest days of my life. On a large open parade ground covered with plush green grass, Company B of the First Infantry Regiment passed in review before a crowd of officers and family members as graduates of the Fort Ord basic training program. And right in the middle of those perfectly aligned rows of very disciplined soldiers marched Donald Huard, in full dress uniform with "Ike" jacket and blue trim, rifle angled just right, snapping his head right on command as he passed the reviewing stand just like in the movies.

I had made it. Now I was part of that fighting machine. Not bad for a 115 lb. kid from the desert who, three months earlier, was afraid of being away from home, afraid to go to sleep at night, afraid of the sound of weapons, afraid of life. Master Sergeant Willy Jenkins, a huge black man with the most powerful voice I had ever heard, yelled the perfect cadence above the sound of the marching band that day, one of the best days of my life!

Sure enough, my first orders were for FECOM. That meant Far East Command. That meant Korea. First, however, eight glorious days on leave, back in Phoenix, Arizona with the sweet smell of orange blossoms, mom's macaroni and tomato soup, much chop suey over mashed potatoes, the drive-in movies with my girlfriend and sleeping in until 10 o'clock in the mornings before mom gently "nudged" me awake for T V and breakfast.

I didn't tell mom and dad right away where I was going. I just didn't want to talk about it for awhile. When it was time to leave, I told them what they already knew. Looking back on it now, I have to admit that basic training in the army was good for me. I was shaken from my sad feelings of self-pity over losing my sweetheart a few months earlier. I learned in a hurry what a great family life I had and how much mom and dad catered to their children. I was forced to accept rigid discipline that bordered on the ridiculous with inspections by officers I learned to fear but came to respect.

I learned how welcome a letter from home could be. Most of all, having met my responsibility to survive and to produce, I was on the way to developing some self-confidence and a feeling that, after all, there was some hope for the skinny kid from the desert.

When I finished my sixteen weeks of light and heavy weapons infantry basic training, I didn't know what the future would hold for me. Would I be sent to actually fight in the war? Was it really a war at all? Many referred to the Korean conflict as a police action, undeclared as a war. Nonetheless, I could be asked to kill others or even to die for my country.

Still, I was proud of my achievement of mere survival of the training. Not bad for one who was so frail as a raw kid draftee, one pulled away from home at such an early age, one who was forced to prove himself capable of becoming a disciplined soldier ready to handle a soldier's potential challenges.

I felt a little more confident about myself after ending my military training, feeling that, after all, there just might be some hope for the 115 lb. Private Donald Huard, a graduate infantryman in Company B of the 6th Division of the United States Army.

CHAPTER TWO

FLOATING AND FLYING - 1953

I returned from my glorious eight day leave in Phoenix to a military base in the Presidio of San Francisco as instructed on my orders. I stayed away just about as long as I could get away with. If I had waited until any time after midnight that Sunday night I would have been A.W.O.L. I checked in just an hour before the deadline. The new sergeant checked to find my name on his guest list then said, "It's gonna be cold where you're going, private Hoaerd." Like all of the other sergeants, who called me Hurd, Hoored, Howard, Etc. Nobody ever got it right. "Yes sir, I know," I answered. I must have had the look of the doomed on my face. "It's very cold in Alaska," he said. "ALASKA!," I yelled. He responded, "Oh, you're another one who didn't get the word that your orders have been changed. You are not going to Korea."

I worked my way through dozens of other soldiers all excitedly trying to get to a telephone to call home to break the good news. "I'm going to ALASKA," I screamed into the phone, awakening mom and dad in the middle of the night. Sure enough, in a few days I was aboard the U.S.S. Jefferson, a rusty WW II troop ship headed for an incredible adventure amidst the glaciers and the Eskimos.

As it turned out, while we were all on leave with our orders for Korea, a general somewhere needed a company of GIs to serve as a supply unit for a private company contracted to survey large parts of Alaska preparatory to its becoming America's next state. The company was called the Coastal Geodetic Survey Company and our infantry regiment was linked to the 30th Engineer's Base Topographical Battalion. We were assigned as a support unit for the surveyors. From then on, we all wore the castle-like *Imprimus* army engineer patches on our Ike jackets.

A little background material about the history of the Alaskan Peninsula can be useful at this point. Alaska occupies the most northwestern portion of the North American Continent. Farther west, across fifty-one miles of the Bering Strait is the Cukotsku Peninsula of the Soviet Union. During the 1800s, Alaska was called Russian America before the United States bought the right to the area from Russia for a negotiated purchase price of $7.3 million, about eight cents per acre. The transfer of Alaska to the U. S. occurred just after the Civil War in 1867. It remained a U.S. territory for the remainder of the century and up through the Second World War. In 1953, young Don Huard arrived to help survey the land, resulting in the acceptance by President Eisenhower of Alaska in 1959 as the 49th American state.

The five-day trip aboard the U.S.S. Jefferson was fine for me for about one half of the first day at sea. On the second day I began to yearn for the hills of Korea. Never before (or since, for that matter) have I ever been so cold, sick and incapacitated. I learned very soon that a ship at sea does not simply float along in a straight line to its destination. Instead, it sways its way from side to side, nose going up and down, its passengers getting sicker and sicker with each creak and groan of the ancient timbers in its belly. I heaved for four of the five days. For four horrible days that seemed like a month, I lay in the hold of that torture pit, praying that I wouldn't fall off of the floor. Twice per day we were forced out of the hold, up on deck to "enjoy" (heave into) the sea. Because the ship was swaying from side to side in the rough Bering Sea, when we stood looking to the left or right on a natural parallel line with the deck we could see an alternating wall of water rushing toward us at one moment, then a wall of sky the next. The water looked as though it would wash us overboard, but it didn't. Anyway, we were all too sick to care.

Late in the afternoon of the fifth day the water began to smooth out. Huge glaciers appeared near the shoreline of the Cook Inlet that narrowed its way toward the Alaskan city of Anchorage. The scenery was absolutely incredible! Bolstered by the thought that I might actually get off of that bolt bucket and inspired by what I never dreamed my eyes would ever see, I clicked away with my cheap box camera loaded with black and white film.

Dave, a Kentucky born friend with an enormous southern drawl, was kind enough to carry my duffle bag off of the ship for me. I was too weak to do it myself.

A few hours later we were on a train that slowly went through the beautiful snow-covered mountains. Then, we were loaded onto trucks for transport to Fort Richardson, an army installation on the outskirts of Anchorage.

A few days later, I found myself strapped to a jump seat mounted against the inner wall of a huge C-130 cargo transport plane with forty other soldiers who, along with three H-23 Hiller helicopters, were being sent to a small airstrip in Galena. It was a miniature outpost in a remote area on the Yukon River in Central Alaska.

There we would serve through the summer months as support staff for the Coastal Geodetic surveyors. My specific responsibility became clear in short order. I was given a small airplane, a Cessna 180 and told to keep it in shape to fly. I had never even been in a small airplane before, let alone been expected to serve as a maintenance specialist for one of them. I knew that the propeller was on the front end the stick made it go up and down.

Out of the innards of a Beechcraft Bonanza one day stepped a short young man of twenty-three or so, the man who was to be my pilot on the L-19 Birddog (my Cessna) that I was assigned to maintain. He looked a little like me, weighing in at about 125 lbs.

However, he was only about 5'3" tall. The difference was that he proudly carried first lieutenant's bars on his shoulders and by me he was called "Sir."

I liked my new lieutenant pilot boss right from the start. He could have turned out to be a real nerd. But he didn't. He could have been overly bossy. But he wasn't. He turned out to be a real nice kid with lots of smarts, a competent, friendly personality and, most important of all, he was a natural as a bush pilot. We risked our necks together in that airplane sometimes that summer and I always felt confident in his ability to get us safely back on the runway. Many of our landings were on dirt clearings and sandbars in the wilds next to surveyor camps where men waited for us to bring in supplies and welcomed mail from home. Some of those landings were very dangerous. I think we made a pretty good team.

All around our "home base" of Galena, with its 10,000 foot runway suitable for landing jet fighters and cargo planes, there were small surveyor camps with men living in tents heated with oil stoves. The camps were on high plateaus or next to river beds or in dirt clearings from which the small helicopters transported crews to remote areas to do their work.

Our job with the Birddog was to keep the copters supplied with fuel and parts, the crews supplied with food, water and the ever important mail from loved ones back home. To do this we took off and landed, at considerable peril, from very short, rough runways carved in the wilderness.

My little lieutenant became extremely skilled at "plopping" our overloaded L-19 onto a cleared runway and getting it stopped just before we hit the trees or went for a swim. We were in and out of camps at places called Kaltag, Nulato, Ruby (the hotspot for Klondike Kate during the late 1800s gold rush days) and McGrath. At the end of each day we returned to the long smooth runway at Galena and the quonset huts used for our barracks away from home.

We considered ourselves lucky to be in those huts rather than in tents. At least they had some solid walls and a little insulation against the cold. At least we were near the "town," a community that had a population of say, twenty elderly Eskimos, a dozen Huskie dogs and an isolated post office. There were no young people, no pretty girls in brightly colored dresses, no Burger King Restaurants for us along the Yukon River. Just military olive drab and more military olive drab. And loneliness for our girlfriends and our families, in my case way back in Phoenix Arizona.

In the midst of winter, there is little daylight in Alaska, maybe only several hours each day. In the midsummer, there is very little darkness. We had arrived in Galena in mid-April when the long winter nights were about over and the weather was warming for a bit. The mosquito population was in the zillions requiring us to work on our planes wearing head nets and gloves. It became difficult to sleep in June and July when there was little darkness. Our work days grew longer as the weeks went by, as the crews were under pressure to do as much surveying as possible before the next winter set in and we were reluctantly(?) required to return to San Francisco. The pressures of bush flying over extremely rugged terrain, getting in and out of dangerous airstrips amidst trees and on sandbars left pilots and crews exhausted at day's end. So much so that late in the afternoon of one August day my pilot fell asleep at the stick while making a landing at Galena!

Sitting in the back of the plane as we approached the runway, I noticed that we seemed a little too high for our usual landing approach. I then noticed a few of the helicopter mechanics down on the deck as they began to wave frantically at us "You're too high. You're too high!"

I slammed my hand against the back of the pilot's seat. When the lieutenant came to the realization that we had landed on the wrong end of the runway headed in the wrong direction and we were going off of the end down into a deep ravine, he awakened in a hurry, but it was too late. So much for U.S. Army 2825, one L-19

Birddog that never flew again. We both climbed out of our severely broken airplane but were luckily uninjured. I never flew with the young lieutenant again after that. I don't know what ever happened to him. He was a great pilot. I hope he was able to keep on flying.

A helicopter pilot and a crew chief, who was a good friend of mine, were killed that summer when for some unknown reason the main rotor blade of their copter came off in flight. They didn't stand a chance of survival. I did a little more growing up that day as I helped to carry the bodies in blood-soaked blankets for loading into a Navy SA-16 amphibious plane for transport back to Anchorage. I remember my first sergeant saying to me, "It's all part of life, kid. It's all part of life." It was a part I had not seen until then.

In October, as the days grew short again, we and the helicopters were loaded back into the C-130s and shipped back to Anchorage. Within days we were afloat again for our five day, not quite so seasick trip aboard the sister-troop ship U.S.S. Jackson back to one of the most beautiful sights that a homesick American soldier can ever feast his eyes on, the image looming larger and larger the closer that you get, of the San Francisco Golden Gate Bridge.

At the base of that bridge is the Presidio of California, Fort Winfield Scott is located there and there is a small airstrip used by the aviation detachment of the 30th Engineer's Base Topographical Battalion. It wasn't Phoenix. It wasn't chop suey over mashed potatoes prepared by mom, but it meant cable cars and movie theaters. It meant young girls in pretty dresses. It meant relief from olive drab. It meant the end of another chapter, a time in my life when I was establishing a bit of independence from my family while on an adventure that could happen only once in a lifetime, or so I thought. Little did I know at the time that I was to spend a second tour the following year assigned more aircraft maintenance responsibility in the same little village of Galena, just next to the Yukon River.

On sometimes dangerous trips to the remote areas being surveyed I would carry a .45 Colt semi-automatic sidearm meant for protection should our airplane go down in a survivable crash. I couldn't hit anything with it, but I felt more secure against the huge bears roaming in the wild forests amidst all kinds of smaller animals. Imagining myself stranded at night in the cold, waiting for the sound of a rescue helicopter, I came to understand why I was being paid several bucks extra per month as hazardous duty pay. "Maybe," I thought, "I might have been safer in Korea, after all."

CHAPTER THREE

BEAVER LOVE – 1954

At last, the army was going to teach me how to work on airplanes, well after I had been doing so for the last six months, risking my own neck and that of my pilot as well. They took me from the comfort of my own home in Phoenix when I was just a boy out of high school, beat the hell out of me for six months, sent me to that place so cold my fingers would crack, then assigned me an airplane and said "Fix it." There's much to the often spoken words, "There's the right way and then there's the army way."

I have to admit, it was better by far than Korea. Even safer than Korea, in spite of my lack of skills. It was my familiarity with grease, oil, spark plugs, filters, wheel bearings, carburetors and busted knuckles that saved me. Most of the time I learned by doing things accidently right. Sometimes, I did actually know what I was doing, surviving the summer quite well except for the price of one airplane that was destroyed by someone else's error. That poor well-trained lieutenant! He made one mistake and it cost the army an expensive airplane. Poor fellow, what a tough break!

My next orders, once back at the mainland were fulfilled through the winter of 1953-54 at Kelly Airforce Base in San Marcos, Texas to be trained as a fixed-wing aircraft frame and engine mechanic. It was nice and warm there. I learned how to prop-start an L-16 without losing my head, just like cranking my old Chevy, except that you had to duck. I *did* follow instructions that time, knowing that if I was struck by the spinning propeller I would die!

The schooling took about eight weeks, during which time much of what I was learning was just old hat to a veteran pro. Some of it, however, was quite fascinating. I learned about magnetos, engine breakdown and reassembly. I learned a lot about fuel systems and the problems pilots and crew faced when they had to fly at higher altitudes to clear mountain terrain. We learned about survival techniques in case we went down and had to be located either during the day or at night. We learned about parachutes and I learned how to pray.

There was absolutely nothing interesting about San Marcos itself. We were confined to the base except for weekends, then encouraged to keep out of the local night spots, many of which had signs on the doors, "Soldiers and dogs keep out." I did my job, learned as much as I could, stayed out of any trouble and looked forward to the trip back to San Francisco as it meant a few days in Phoenix on the way.

In Phoenix, I visited with family, dated my girlfriend Kathy, visited with her folks (whom I liked) and spent a couple of days hunting for a used car to take back to the base. I ended up with a 1950 Olds 88 sedan that was sharp and hot and two-toned blue.

Out of basic training and with a little more freedom in San Francisco, I began to make some friends, notably because I was the one who had a nice car. Although painfully shy about "foreign" girls, I double-dated a few times and became familiar with the young party set. I was, however, never really comfortable with a drink in my hand. I seemed relaxed only when I was working on my L-19 or my Olds, never when I had to socialize with the "with it" crowd.

Then, there was the shape-up program sponsored by some macho colonel who was trying to impress some general with the spit and polish of his troops. We stood at attention in the barracks for endless stupid inspections and military discipline. I hated that nonsense with a passion. It was too much like going to confession as required by mom back in my youth. Besides, one smart-assed captain actually asked me if I had stolen my uniform because it was too big for me. Those Ike jackets only came so small and, remember, I was a very skinny kid.

As winter returned to spring, plans were again being made for more summer surveying with the Coastal Geodetic Group. We did special inspections on our aircraft preparing them for the heavy work ahead. One day, Sergeant Moriarty called me into his maintenance office and told me that I had been selected to be a crew-chief on a larger plane. The plane was a DeHaveland Beaver, called the Army L-20. Furthermore, said my boss, "You are going to be one of the fellows who will fly in the plane to Alaska, then on to Galena."

That meant several things to me. One was that I had earned a step up in responsibility by doing a good job on the L-19 during the preceding summer. The second was that I would have an assistant to boss around (he was an Italian kid who was most helpful). He was a funny guy who laughed like a donkey. Third, I would not have to spend five days up and five days back violently seasick on the U.S.S. Boltbucket!

That L-20 was something else! Man, how I learned to love that airplane! However, the army did it to me again. Having been trained belatedly on how to take care of a small Cessna L-19 that I had already worked on for six months, the brass sent me back to Galena to work on a different kind of airplane with no training on it either. While the L-19 was a tandem two-seater with the pilot up front and the passenger behind him, powered by a 180 horse-powered six cylinder opposed Continental engine, the "Beaver" was a six passenger plane with a nine cylinder 450 horse-powered Pratt Whitney radial engine. It was supercharged, and so was I! It even had a variable pitch prop! In that one, I sat next to my pilot, acting as his co-pilot.

Now, I've been saying that I hated the army, that I had a remarkable hate relationship with anything and everything military.

That airplane was the exception to the rule. To this day, I adore that airplane. I have actually considered getting a license to fly and buying one of those airplanes! Obviously, I'm going to have much to say about that plane.

The Beaver is a boxy looking, squarish looking plane, round only at the front cowling over its great big engine. Mine was white with red trim with U.S. Army 2813 painted on its rudder and "LUCKY THIRTEEN" on its nose. The interior of the plane was wide enough for me to sit crew-chief aside of one of the neatest people I ever knew, my pilot, Captain Paul Hopkins. There were four seats behind us used by traveling brass or other personnel. We often removed those rear seats to make the plane into a cargo carrier. It was the perfect vehicle for short strip take-offs and landings at the dirt runways cleared in the wilds. Many of the used ones are still being used today in the jungles or with floats on lakes all over the world. Harrison Ford even crashed a Beaver in one of his recent movies. His co-star, Anne Hecht wanted him to "glue" it back together.

Riding in one, behind the roar of that radial engine is a real adventure. The engine has what is called an "inertia" starter. What that means is that unlike an automobile that has its starter connected directly to the engine, the plane uses its battery to energize a heavy flywheel that whines louder and louder, increasing in RPMs until it is suddenly engaged so that the heavy weight of the spinning wheel can crank the engine. If you are lucky, it starts with a monstrous roar.

Radial engines run notoriously rough when they first start and are at low RPMs. The airframe shakes, the engine sputters, backfires and chokes on the full rich mixture of fuel needed to get it running. When the throttle is advanced slowly and the fuel mixture is leaned out, the power becomes smooth at about 1000 RPMs and as a motor-lovin' kid from Phoenix, I would go into orbit each time. I was absolutely enthralled by the power. It was like being on a set of rails at the local drag strip. I nearly peed with excitement whenever we took that thing off.

In early April of 1954, I sat in the back of Lucky 13 behind a couple of very capable military pilots as we took off on the first leg of a most exciting trip through Canada, the Yukon territory and into Alaska. The first stop was in Elco, Nevada. We stayed over night in a hotel and were treated to a fabulous meal as though we were royal guests.

The next day we flew to Butte, Montana where we had to land in a fifty mile per hour crosswind. It took repeated attempts before we could get glued to the runway. Each time we were about to touch down, a gust of wind would lift us up and throw us to the right or left. A wise captain used a clever technique I had seen my L-19 pilot use in the mountains near Galina the year before. He intentionally came in with the flaps down, waiting until just the right time to yank up on the lever and take all of the flight out of the aircraft. He essentially crashed the aircraft in and prayed that we would stay down on the runway. It worked. I, of course, was not nervous at all, being the veteran crew-chief that I was...

From Butte, it was into Canada with our next stop at Calgary, then on to Edmonton, Alberta where another hotel stay was made interesting by the activity of our officers in the room next to us, having what sounded to us like a very fine time with a few very noisy women. One of the perks of Officer's Candidate School, I guess. Enlisted men, of course, were not included.

We flew seven airplanes in squadron formations, two of the larger Beavers and five L-19s with pilots radioing back and forth as we cruised over the green rolling hills of western Alberta. The air was smooth, the scenery inspiring, surely this was a better way to travel than the floor-clinging naval adventure of the last year.

We landed next at Dawson Creek, a very small outpost with an aviation fuel station, a few villagers and just about nothing else. It was getting colder the farther north that we went and we seemed to get farther and farther from civilization. Another day's flying brought us to White Horse in the Yukon Territory. where we got weathered in for a few extra days.

After a short fuel stop at St. John, before leaving the Yukon over some very treacherous mountains we settled into Anchorage. It was a splendid adventure for a kid from the desert. I was quite proud to be the crew-chief on one of the bigger planes, one of the supercharged radial engine planes, one with a variable pitch prop and the sound of a DC-3. After a few day's rest we headed for my old stompin' grounds at Galena.

Flying from Anchorage to Galena involved risking our lives when we traveled in aircraft light enough to be thrown this way and that by the buffeting air currents naturally produced by wind ricocheting off of majestic mountains. Our only stop in-between was at McGrath. To get us to that location we had to climb to an altitude of over 10,000 feet and go through a mountain pass next to Mt. McKinley that had become famous among Alaskan bush pilots for its tendency to gobble up light aircraft. We actually saw the wreckage of several that had not made it through the narrow passageway. Our anxiety levels increased to the point of nausea. I began to vomit. I was not the only one.

At that level, a light non-pressurized airplane is near its flying ceiling. The laboring engines, notably on the L-19s without superchargers were starved for oxygen, some of them overheating even in the frigid cold. The scenery was spectacular! Even the word -spectacular- could not describe the wonder and beauty before our eyes as we passed within a few thousand yards of the peak of Mt. McKinley. I felt as John Glenn must have felt when he was on his orbital space flight around the earth in 1962, as though I was sharing the wonders of creation in the presence of God.

Once through the pass and into smoother air, we began to relax, anticipating our arrival at Galena. Galena was well, what can I say, just Galena. It wasn't a tourist's town by any measure. Just like the year before, it was too cold, then too hot, too humid, too dark, then too bright and terribly lonely. Again, I craved anything that had color to it. Except for the red and white of our airplanes, everything else was drab, the runway, the thousands of fifty-five gallon gasoline and oil drums, the empty hangers, the boredom, the waiting for letters from home...

I remember one day in mid-summer when a commercial airliner stopped at our airstrip to refuel. A door opened and for a magnificent half-hour a lovely lady stewardess in a plum-colored uniform stood on the ramp at the top of the stairs. Fueling the Beaver, fifty yards away, I couldn't stop looking at her. "What in hell am I doing here in drabsville," I asked myself? The vision of her made me feel even more lonely for the colors, the sweet smell of my girlfriend's cologne and the orange blossoms at home.

But there was work to be done. My portion of it was to keep that Beaver in operating condition, keep my capable pilot safe and happy and to help with the difficult task of supplying the helicopter crews and surveyors with many of the things they needed to do *their* jobs. So we were soon on our daily routines, mine involving the servicing, fueling and warming up of the engine and loading and belting in of the nervous passengers or anchoring cargo down before my pilot would arrive for each flight. Sometimes I would go along, sometimes not.

My considerate pilot became a special friend, a mentor. He was a second "dad" to me for most of the remaining months I served in the military. He commanded more respect from the enlisted men there than the others, even some of higher rank. I couldn't say exactly why. There was something about him, something about his strong confident personality and his natural control over even the most critical situations that gained respect from the men who worked with him.

The captain was a reserve officer, called back into the service during the Korean War after having served as a pilot in Europe in WW II. He was in his late thirties, a tall striking looking man who usually appeared neater than a hard day's flying would permit. He had a partial gold front tooth that added a little class to his look, a clear strong voice that was gentle, unless he got mad. Then, look out! I heard him chew out a few recruits from time to time and he was a real pro. Yet, in spite of a few times when he perhaps should have, he never came down on me. I think he knew how hard I was trying. Perhaps he had a son like me. I don't know.

When my pilot flew *my* ship, he always treated it as though he were on his way to church with his family. Easy does it, use only the power needed, use almost all of the available runway, climb slowly, gently... Start descending miles away from the landing site, touch down with a delicate flair. What a classy guy!

His inspections of the aircraft as preflights or after scheduled maintenance by my crew and me were most thorough. He wouldn't fly if he found even the slightest problem. No "we'll catch it after the next flight" kind of thing for him. He expected us to be always on our toes and we were. Almost always.

Once my assistant left a cotter key out of the tail wheel assembly resulting in the airplane "wobbling" a bit while taxiing. The boss didn't detect it, but one of us noticed it first. We corrected that one in a hurry. Then, there was the time when I was beside the captain on a post maintenance test flight at about 6,000 feet above Galena when suddenly there was a blast of air that hit us from the back, causing the plane to buffet and shake as we came out of a shallow dive. We were only about 150 miles from the Soviet border in Galena and with the cold war on we were ever on the alert for the possibility that we might get too close and offend the Russians.

The first thing we thought of when that blast hit us was that we had been hit by a missile from a Soviet jet. My amazing pilot worked to get control and he actually told me that we might have to parachute down. I got ready to get out, hoping that I wouldn't get clobbered by any of the tail section on the way down. As he slowed our airspeed from about 140 knots down to 100, the buffeting eased, then stopped. In a surprisingly calm, but characteristic manner, he said, "It's okay, I've got it. At ease, soldier," to the most terrified kid west of the Pecos - *me!*

"Mayday, Mayday," we radioed to the emergency crew on the deck. But our landing was perfectly routine. We were followed to the maintenance area by several trucks. When we got out we couldn't find anything wrong! Then suddenly my assistant's big head popped out of the top of ole' Lucky 13 where a small window was missing from above the pilot's seat.

We doped it out later. When we were pulling out of that dive, the vacuum over the top of the plane pulled out one of the twin observation windows just above the pilot's head. That, in turn, created a vacuum in the passenger compartment that suddenly drew air from the rear, blasting open a rear baggage compartment, hitting us from the back of the craft causing it to buffet wildly. There was no Soviet threat, no missile, no airframe damage and I, being my calm, self-assured self, had dealt with the situation in a most mature, and routine manner.

CHAPTER FOUR

A HAPPY DAY, THEN ONE NOT SO - 1953

An occasional happy day, or at least one that starts happy, will break the gloom-cycle for awhile, and one I remember occurred on May 9th, 1954. Several good things happened that day. I turned twenty-one on that day. Also, some orders came through, one of which assigned me to hazardous duty pay and, therefore, I would get $50 more per month for risking a life that was worth about that much. Another was a report of my promotion to the rank of corporal. Altogether, I would find my paycheck bringing me about $175 more each month. Now, *that's* a happy day!

Got to celebrate, right? Well, celebrate is what I did. I damned near killed myself with alcohol! At the urgings of my peers, I started drinking beer early in the evening. Not being accustomed to the arts, I started to get wobbly about an hour later. Then, when I should have quit, I let those who were to blame (because I never am) talk me into having a few more beers and then a few more.

When I staggered out of the hall, I kept falling and was picked up by my trusty buddies. Then, we passed the aircraft control tower. For some reason unknown to myself (I found this out the next day), I began to throw full cans of beer at the tower. Fortunately, it was too tall for my range and too narrow for my aim. In the process, however, I fell hard on a remaining can of beer that was in a pocket of my field jacket severely bruising a rib or two. Eventually I was thrown into a

25

Jeep and pitched out onto the dirt in front of our quonset hut, where, crawling inside, I slept off one of the worst experiences of my young life. Not recommended.

In the morning, when my pilot went down to the flight line, he found his airplane still cold and unfueled. His dedicated crew-chief was nowhere in sight. He tracked me down. Finding me moaning and heaving on my cot, he took pity on his miserable subordinate. His only comment was, "Huard, if there had been a good woman, you'd be dead this morning."

That was one time that he really could have reamed my tail if he had felt so inclined, but he didn't. Then, there was another time, and it was one that had extremely serious implications. In fact, I will feel my anxiety level increase now as I write about what happened one day when I let my guard down and almost caused five people to lose their lives. Had the Lord not been with me that day, I could be carrying the guilt for those deaths. I could have been held up for possible court marshal and been convicted of negligent homicide and sent for decades to a military prison.

Let me set the stage for what happened. Occasionally the big brass would come to Galina to view the troops. That meant that my busy Beaver had to be scrubbed and prepped for their flights out to the tent camps where the surveying was being done. There were seven or eight of those camps on various hilltops, sand bars and plateaus. The top whig and his assistant officers included a full bird colonel, a major, a captain and a no-named lieutenant.

The colonel was just one step down from the rank of brigadier general. So, as you might imagine, this was a day when we all trembled a bit, like the day when the priest was coming to visit our fourth grade class at St. Al's after a week of "fear conditioning" by the sisters. We had prepared for a week for the arrival of those executive officers from Elmendorf Air Force Base, the base near Anchorage.

I saw to it that my work-horse of an airplane was spotless that day. I filled the tanks, checked the oil over and over again, aired the tires to within a tenth of a tenth of a pound of recommended pressure, etc. All seats were in place, all parachutes were arranged with the sparkling latches perfectly placed. The polished seat belt buckles were positioned with disgusting military precision, with shoulder harnesses ready to be latched around the high monarch and his aides.

When they arrived, I stood at attention until my captain told me to help board the brass. After awhile, everyone in place, I saluted at attention as my pilot taxied to the runway. Soon, using the full length of the runway, the captain gently raised the Beaver's nose and I watched as the full power was on for takeoff and was thrilled to see the plane get smaller and smaller as they headed for Kaltag. I listened as the full power was on for takeoff and felt excited by the smooth whine of that incredible engine. You would have thought that I was listening to Mozart, as did Solieri, enraptured by the splendor of the eloquent sound.

No more than a half hour or so later, I heard something very strange off in the distance. It was a sound both familiar and different at the same time. It was the whine of my Beaver, but punctuated by big explosions about every five to seven seconds or so. "Whirr, BANG, whirr, BANG, whirrrrrrr, BANG, whirr, BANG!" Something was seriously wrong! I watched and listened nervously. Then I began to pray that they would make it to the end of the runway. I was terrified that they might crash into the pines or into the rows of the gas drums nearby.

Soon, with the engine backfiring and struggling, they taxied up to where I was waiting and the pilot shut the engine down. I watched as the badly shaken officers climbed out and retreated into the nearby hanger. Each must have communicated with his maker that day.

I climbed under the plane and checked the gas drainage sump valve to see if, by some terrible error, there could be water in the aviation fuel. I was absolutely stunned when water poured out of that valve! Lots of water! I knew immediately that I was in lots of trouble, *really* big trouble!

In order to make this meaningful, I should explain how light aircraft were normally fueled in the field in those days. We had to pump 100 octane gasoline from fifty-five gallon drums by using a hand operated pump. It was very hard work. It takes a long time to fill an eighty gallon tank. The gas was pumped into the bowl of a big funnel that had to be covered with an equally large chamois (like the one you would use to dry off your car) which absorbs any water that might be going into the tank. We always "shammied" the gas, usually finding that our supply drums had little water.

That day it was different. Apparently, I had pumped gas from one drum that had water. Previously I had pumped hundreds of drums and never got water anything like what I got that day. And, against a routinely used practice, I guess I didn't use a shammy. I still cannot believe it! Of all days to screw up...

Soon, several officers were out near the plane asking me what was wrong. Being the young, naive stupid honest kid that I was, I confessed that there was water in the gas. I could have loosened a wire on a magneto or on an electric fuel pump. I could have pinched a fuel line. I could have found a scuffed rotor. I could have "tricked" a number of things, but not for me, not for young, dumb, honest Corporal Huard. All my life I had been taught to confess... Like my totally honest hardware store dad, I humbly opted for the truth.

One of the officers, a major, exploded into a rage, stood me up against a hanger wall at attention and proceeded to curse me, verbally thrashing me with his snarling face inches away from mine It went on and on. I don't know how long it took, but I know it was a long time. I stood at attention, dying inside and trying not to show it. crying, but trying to be an army corporal and not letting him see me cry. That major broke me that day. Frail as I was when I was drafted into the army, basic training couldn't break me. Five days of sea sickness couldn't break me. But that major did.

Strangely, my pilot never said a word to me about that incident. I can't express how much I appreciated his silence. He had good reason to take me apart, but he didn't. He must have known how much I was hurting. He will always be gentle on my mind. For some very special reasons, I held greater respect for Captain Paul Hopkins than for any other man I ever met in my brief life up to that time, except for my own dad, of course, my dear too honest dad. "Why did you have to teach me to be so honest, Pop?"

For the next few months I tried to put some meaning into that experience. I thanked God over and over that no one had died because of my carelessness. I traced my every step that morning over and over again in my consciousness. I knew that I had shammied that gas. I always did. How could there have been as much as a gallon of water in that sump? What were the odds of getting my first bad barrel on that specific day? I've never been able to answer those questions. Did someone else intentionally try to down my aircraft when it was to be loaded with all of those high level officers?

Did someone pour a gallon of water into the tank the night before? I know I shammied that gas. I would swear on the Bible that I shammied that gas. I will never know. What a tragedy that would have been!

What would have happened if my highly skilled pilot had not been able to safely land Corporal Donald Huard's sputtering DeHaviland Beaver on that fateful morning? What would have happened if the airplane filled with army officers had crashed into the pines before reaching the runway? Over the last sixty years I have repeatedly asked myself that question. Would all aboard have been killed? Would six families have suffered the loss of their fathers, sons or brothers as a result of Don Huard's failure to keep water out of the plane's gasoline?

Surely, an investigation would have been conducted following such a tragedy. Is it likely that twenty year-old draftee Corporal Huard would have faced possible court marshal to be tried for manslaughter or negligent homicide? If convicted, would I have ended up in a military stockade or federal prison? For how many years?

A staff sergeant fellow in our maintenance crew was always angrily expressing his hatred for officers. I suspected that he might have intentionally tried to sabotage my plane during the night before, but I was afraid to accuse him of any complicity. I had no proof. So, I said nothing.

However, I knew that I *had* shammied the gasoline that I pumped into the Beaver tank. I *always* did. I can still hear the backfiring of that big radial engine as I prayed that they would make it onto the runway. Thank God! They made it! Thank God that what could have happened - didn't!

With my confidence slowly recovering over the next months, I continued to do my job. Very carefully. I built a barrel rack and "engineered" a way that my pilot could "bomb" the tent camps with two half-filled drums of gasoline to be used in the 'copters. A jet canopy release worked as a bomb release, the barrels being dropped into the rivers and lakes near the camps so that they wouldn't burst when they hit. My pilot learned to drop those drums in the water and actually bounce them up on the shore. This eliminated the need to make dangerous landings with drums of gas on board.

As the long days grew shorter near summer's end we prepared for the flight home. Somebody wanted to know if anyone knew anything about picture-taking. I volunteered and found myself as the official flight photographer with a brand new 16 mm movie camera and all of the film I could eat. I shot roll after roll making a documentary film of our trip. *That* was great fun. Somewhere in the archives of the aviation detachment of the 30th Engineer's Base Topographical Battalion of the U.S. Army there's a technicolor film of that trip, our take offs, flight formations over the vast snow-covered mountains and our landings. But I never did see the film - the film taken by Corporal Donald Huard. Damn, that's neat!

We traveled down to McGrath, then through that treacherous

pass next to Mt. McKinley again, and on to Anchorage. Then, down pass in the Yukon Territory. I sat side by side with my special pilot as we flew through the entire western portion of the country of Canada. There we were in late September, looking off in the distance for our first glimpse of the approaching treasure, the Golden Gate Bridge. Soon, home was in sight! For the last time, I reached for the intercom mike and spoke with Captain Paul, "Thanks for getting me home safe, Sir," I said. Do you know what he said to me? "Thanks for keeping it flying, corporal. You did a good job." This, in spite of the fact that I had nearly cost him his life. Or, *had* I? I'll never know. His wife and kids were at the runway, waiting for us (him) when we touched down. I wanted to tell his kids that their dad was the greatest pilot in the world. But, soon they were gone. A soldier showed up in a Jeep to get the camera and the many rolls of film I had shot. I never saw Captain Paul again.

Fifty-two days later, I was on the road to Los Angeles to hug my sister Shirley before heading to Phoenix. It was dark when I got to her apartment. She was just walking up the street after getting off the bus from work. Seeing her, I yelled "Hi Red," and she snubbed me, thinking that I was just another fellow flirting with a pretty girl. "Hi, it's Don," I said. And then I got my hug. I've often wondered if she remembers that day, when I was once again, a free man.

The L-20 "Beaver" - My Love Galena, Alaska – 1954

When I *did* shammy the gasoline...

CHAPTER FIVE

"CONGRATULATIONS, DON." WELCOME TO ACADEMIA.

Dr. H. Clay Skinner, the elderly chairman of the psychology department at the University caught me coming down the stairs of the old Lycium building one morning. He extended his hand out to me and sent me into a panic that buckled my knees. I didn't have the slightest idea why he was being so kind to this lowly graduate student with my new master's degree and a little teaching experience, one just beginning as a new psychology lecturer.

"Sir," I asked, am I in trouble? What have I done?" "Oh", the doctor said. "Don, you are to be the first of the doctoral candidates in our new program to present your master's thesis to the department staff and your fellow graduate students as the featured symposium speaker of the month."

"Oh, my God," I thought. I can't do that! I've got to get out of this in some way, any way I can.. I had better re-enlist in the army or plan a coronary attack or get the flu or break a leg or something to escape from a gig like that! But, there was no way out. I felt trapped, *terrified* was a word that fit. "How could I ever face that crowd? What's a symposium? How did I ever get into that mess?"

Two weeks later I saw several brochures on bulletin boards on campus advertising my day of reckoning. "Donald Huard, M.A. will present his master's thesis research at 3:00 P. M. on Oct. 23, 1959 in the department of psychology... My presentation lasted an hour and was quite well received. Afterward, I was applauded (an experience that was new to me) and complimented for my speaking ability and the methods I had employed in data collection and analysis. Professor Haigh said to me, "Don, you should be a *teacher.*" Dr. Carolyn Staats, a social science researcher was later quoted as saying, "If Don is an example of our prospective candidates, we won't have to worry about being a second-rate school." Coffee and doughnuts were presented to the forty or so who attended, including professors of psychology and philosophy and a dozen fellow graduate students. What an ego-boosting experience for the new lecturer, the skinny kid from the desert!

The reason for my emphasis on that experience goes beyond just my feeling of personal accomplishment on that day. I write about it because I want to stress the fact that I had become a highly qualified graduate student with three degrees by that time, a time that was followed a few years later by my being treated as a substandard student, insulted and humiliated by two senior professors in that same University department.

Doctor Skinner, that pleasant elderly department chairman died several years later at a time when I was working for him as an assistant teacher. Just days after his death, I was asked to finish out the semester with his students, becoming a lecturer as his replacement. The following semester I was assigned two of my own classes and for several years after that I taught day and evening classes at the University.

To me it was an honor to be the only graduate student in the department who taught in the new sloped-down lecture hall with its center stage suitable for communication with as many as 140 young adults at a time. It was at that time that I decided I wanted a teaching career. Especially when teaching large evening classes, often including folks in their fifties and sixties, I would thrive on discussions about my career, my family, my kids and my dreams, notably my plan to finish my doctorate program. Occasionally, I even discussed what was in our textbook, what was supposed to be the real subject matter for the course.

I felt special. All of those people getting together to hear wisdom from Donald Huard. It was like the way I felt as the crew chief in the military assigned to maintain a big Dehaviland Beaver with its supercharged engine while the other crew chiefs worked only on the smaller Cessnas. In front of those big classes at the University, *I* was supercharged!

However, I was to learn eventually that even in the world of academia at the predoctoral level some aspiring students run into obstacles that prevent their progression toward the completion of their programs. There came a time a few years later when my own position in the psychology department changed, and not for the better. Something I said or something I did resulted in severe criticism that had a blocking effect on my plan to complete the requirements for my doctorate degree.

Several professors turned against me and eventually they got some higher level administrators to support their efforts to prevent my progress. The story about what happened will take several of my remaining chapters to tell.

I tried so hard to meet all of the requirements for my degree. There was so much stress, so much debt, so much family responsibility. How could I ever hope that my future would include the fulfilment of a dream, that of becoming a doctor of psychology? Who would try to stop me? Why? I didn't understand what was happening to me. Why was I not being encouraged to get my degree?

Just imagine having a dream, then pursuing that dream with all of the hopeful enthusiasm you can muster, all of the discipline you can tolerate and at whatever price must be paid for fulfillment. You dedicate yourself and seek the support of those who believe in you. You work, work, work over many months and even years to be successful in that endeavor.

Perhaps it's in a sports field, say tennis or gymnastics. Maybe it's in the business world. Maybe it's in your goal to become a skilled surgeon. Whatever it is, you feel a very intense motivation to be the best that you can be. For me, a young military veteran using the G I Bill to begin my study at Phoenix College as a somewhat remedial student getting only C grades, the journey was a long one starting in 1954. In 1956 I met all of the requirements for an associate in arts degree and headed for the state University with a developing interest in the field of psychology. Two years later I had earned my bachelor's degree and in 1959, a master's degree in experimental psychology.

That year, at the age of twenty-seven, I met and became married to a lovely fourth grade teacher who was content to give up her teaching career and join this intense young psychologist in the raising of four children who delighted us, challenged us and rewarded us over a period of twenty-three years. Marie Fournier Huard passed away in 1981 at the age of forty-nine. It was an extremely difficult time for our family when a complicated blood chemistry disease took "Mom" away from her children in their late teens and left them and their devastated father.

I had the great good fortune to marry again, to Margaret Russell Huard, the mother of three children who has enriched my life for the last thirty-six years. In our eighties as this book is being written, we "enjoy" being grand parents and great grand parents of a total of 38 children.

I often look back to the time when Marie and I were parents of four kids under the age of six and desperately in need of income, with mounting debt and most of my time being spent at the University trying to meet the requirements for a Ph.D. degree. I think of the problems we faced in order to fulfill our dream, that of making me into a doctor of psychology. The price to be paid for my success as a graduate student was enormous, having a significant effect on our marriage.

Imagine, if you will, what it would be like to be a person

committed to the dream of becoming a champion tennis star or figure skater, having trained for years only to have your dream thwarted by someone who became determined to prevent your achievement. Imagine a marathon runner in the lead in the big race, exhausted, approaching the finish line who is intentionally "tripped" and knocked to the pavement by someone who wanted him to fail. He would reach up hoping that some one, anyone, would help him, but he would find that no one cared...

Am I painting a picture that is just melodrama, an unlikely scenario or one that is an accurate representation of what happened in the late 1960s to Donald Huard as I attempted to complete the requirements for my Ph.D. degree at the state University?

It will seem strange that this book contains extensive coverage of my very complicated history of conflict with the professors and administrative deans at one of my home state Universities during the closing years of the 1960s and the beginning of the 1970s. After all, the story is almost fifty years old now.

One evening, during the third year of my struggle for a successful completion of my doctorate program in a fair manner, I was forced to admit that the University had won and I had lost all hope of becoming a doctor of psychology. That was after nearly twenty years of preparation with an unblemished record of achievement in study, examination proficiency and even serving as a lecturer for three years in the very department of the University that was rejecting me.

On that specific evening I found my first wife Marie standing in the back yard of our home crying over the fact that our dream had crumbled. She was crushed at seeing me in such depression that I had not realized was significantly affecting not just my academic career, but also my marriage. It was surely affecting my supportive wife who believed in me and had done so for years. "You have not been the same for so long now," she cried. "You have left me out, and I don't know what I can do to help you," she cried. I held her and decided that night that I had to put our family first. For the sake of my family,

I had to quit. I had to face it. I could fight no more. Two professors at my own state University were actively preventing me from doing a required final dissertation to finish my Ph.D. program. I couldn't believe what had happened to me over a period of three years that held me under almost unbearable stress that affected both my career and my marriage.

As you progress through my story you will see that I still couldn't give up. But to this day, I wonder what the cost was to my family. I do know that even now I pay an emotional price for the unprofessional conduct I was subjected to by many professors and deans who conspired to prevent me from getting my degree. Collectively, they conspired to hide their treatment of me from others and even from one another. The story should be as much about them, as it is about me...

This tired old psychology professor owes one very special attorney and a couple of other professors at Arizona State University over $150,000! It's quite amazing, isn't it? Well, it's true. The attorney is gone now. John Morris passed away a few years ago. It's not that I had borrowed that amount of money from Mr. Morris and the others. It's instead, a matter of some kind men coming to the defense of one who was down at a time when their help could make a difference, a really big difference. Attorney John Morris made that difference. Jack Michael and Robert E. Haygood, both Ph.Ds in the psychology department also helped to make that difference. Although fifty years have passed since my rescue, I still feel compelled to tell my story.

It's a very long story, so you will have to be patient. It's a sad story that ends happily. It's a story that has all sorts of lessons in it, you know, like the old "believe in yourself" story. Or maybe the "never give up on your dream" story. "Don't let people push you around," is another story that fits. It can even be seen as a "revenge is a meal best served cold" kind of story.

Hopefully, I won't lose you en route. It's quite likely that it began before you were born. I suppose that it began in about 1956 or 57 or so, after I had been discharged from my service in the army. I worked on washing machines for awhile, then opted to try a few classes at Phoenix Community College without the foggiest idea of what I wanted to do for the long term or even who I wanted to be. To my surprise, I was successful in getting "C"s and a few "B" grades and eventually I graduated with an Associate in Arts degree. Moving on to the state University, I decided to major in psychology.

After an additional two years I had a bachelor's degree. Then, in 1959 I graduated with a master's degree followed by an appointment as a lecturer in the psychology department at the age of twenty-seven. I taught many classes over the next three years, the largest being one with over 140 students. During those years I also worked on fulfilling course work requirements toward my Ph.D. degree. I met my foreign language requirement (French) and established two graduate level minors, one in business and the other in the field of criminal justice.

I accepted a full time teaching position at Phoenix College in 1963 after completing all of the course work and the final comprehensive examinations for the degree. All that remained for me was the need to complete and defend a doctoral dissertation within a five year time period following the passage of the "comps." It seems straight forward enough, doesn't it? The problem at that time was that a full time teaching position at any community college is quite demanding, notably if you are the bread winner in a large family and must work teaching night and summer classes to stay in reasonably good financial shape.

About three and a half years went by before I began to get concerned about having enough time left to finish my program at the University. I wrote a letter to the chairman of the psychology department indicating my intention to complete my work and requested that my graduate committee direct me in my dissertation development. However, I was to learn that my former committee had been canceled, my senior professor had taken a position at the

University of Hawaii. No one was interested in my dissertation project. My letter to the department wasn't even answered.

With only a year of eligibility remaining I decided to go to the psychology department to see if I could get a new committee established. As I spoke with the acting chairman I made the mistake of mentioning that my letter was not answered and he appeared to become quite irritated. He then proceeded to criticize me for "coming on too strong." A personality clash if there ever was one. Our conversation ended with Dr. "Gus" telling me "You'll get no help from me." As chairman of the department, this man was in the position to see to it that I never got my doctor's degree. And so, the saga began. What was I to do? What *could* I do? After all, it took me twenty years to get to the point of completing my program. "Do I just quit," I asked myself? I found myself at the mercy of this man. It was obvious that he disliked me, seeing me as one who was arrogant and undeserving of his support. Had I lost any opportunity to fulfill my dream?

As a military veteran, I knew the importance of following the appropriate chain of command for airing grievances, so on the recommendation of another faculty member I made an appointment to see the dean of the College of Liberal Arts. It was a pleasant meeting with Dean "George," a gentle British sounding man who seemed to be sympathetic with my unfortunate position and my continuing desire to meet the dissertation requirement for the doctor's degree. He then offered to discuss the matter with the psychology chairman in hopes that something could be worked out that would result in the setting up of a new committee and the completion of my program.

Sure enough, two months later I received a letter of concern from the chairman in which he challenged my course work as having been inadequate for the degree, suggesting that I would need to take additional classes under *his* direction and then be retested by a new committee. I would then be required to pass a second comprehensive examination! However, he wrote, "If you would like to present a new dissertation prospectus (proposal) to the department, *I* and two of my colleagues would be willing to evaluate it and if it meets with our approval, we will form a committee and direct you toward the final completion of your program." Feeling that I at least had a shot at doing the dissertation, I worked all summer long writing a prospectus. Little did I know that the chairman would be waiting for it and that he was intent on rejecting it even before he read it! The rejection letter stunned me! I had been set up and shot down by the chairman of the University psychology department. There went my degree! The letter contained several insights into my lack of competency as a candidate at the doctoral level and even revealed some sarcasm in the chairman's tone. What was I to do? What *can* I do? Should I just quit? Should I just let that vindictive man steal so much of my future?

CHAPTER SIX

THE HORNS OF A DILEMMA
DO I QUIT OR DO I DECIDE TO FIGHT?

Are you still with me, dear reader? Do you begin to see my predicament? What would you have done under those circumstances? I made another appointment to see the dean. Again, I found him to be somewhat sympathetic. In fact, as I entered his office he immediately got up from his desk, came up to me said "I saw the chairman's rejection letter, Mr. Hoored (he never did get my name right,) IT WAS BRUTAL!" I indicated to the dean how hurt I was and how unfair I felt the chairman had been. Never to my knowledge, had a doctoral candidate who successfully passed the comprehensive exams been required to repeat them. I pleaded with the dean to arrange a meeting at which we could all discuss this matter. He agreed to do so. The brutality in the letter turned out to be just another painful beginning as I learned something about the phrase "cruel reality."

As I waited for the meeting scheduled for nearly a month later, I wrote to two of my former professors about what was happening to me. I enclosed copies of the letter by the chairman that gave me a chance to submit a prospectus and the one that rejected me. The professor at the University of Hawaii sent one to the dean verifying that I had been a qualified candidate as he worked with me in years past. Needless to say, I appreciated that letter, sent with a carbon copy to me. I had worked for Dr. Staats for two years as I continued with the preparation for my "comps."

Then, a break came for me (I thought at the time) when the phone rang on a Sunday afternoon and I heard the familiar voice of Dr. Jack Michael from the University of Western Michigan. I had worked in close association with "Jack" as he set up his operant conditioning laboratory at the University. I conferred with his students and assisted with lab procedures under his direction for about two years.

"Tell me, Don, what's happening," he asked? I sat right down on the kitchen floor, leaned my back against the base of the refrigerator and poured out my story. It took over a half hour to fill in the details. Dr. Jack made me feel a bit better about things, especially when he said he would think about my problem, while assuring me that I would hear from him in a few days.

Just a week before the scheduled meeting for which I had pleaded, the dean got a very long letter from the U. of W. M. In his letter Dr. Jack pointed out that of the three major criticisms of my prospectus that were used as a basis for rejection, two were unwarranted in light of recent research techniques of which the chairman had been unaware. The third criticism posed only a minor problem that could be corrected with ease. Because Dr. Jack was a member of the editorial board of the leading operant conditioning journal called *The Experimental Analysis of Behavior* or J-Ab, as it was called, there was no denying that, as he put it in the letter, "Mr. Huard's proposal had merit." Yet, it *was* rejected by the chairman. "You'll get no help from me."

I can only imagine how the dean must have felt when he read that letter, knowing that I had a copy to bring up at the scheduled meeting. It was obvious that I had been rejected arbitrarily by several professors who didn't know the literature on which my prospectus was based! Needless to say, armed with Dr. Jack's letter that included some rather flattering comments about my abilities, I was ready to state my case at the meeting.

Do I still have you, my dear and patient readers? Well, hang on, because you are not going to believe what happened during that meeting. When I entered the room, I saw the dean, chairman "Gus" and two other younger professors from the psychology department in a huddle, perhaps anticipating my expressions of concern. The dean introduced me to the young men and then did something very unusual. He stood up and said "I know you all have things to iron out of a technical nature, so I will leave you to discuss them." I saw right away that he was going to throw me to the wolves, so I responded. "Sir, I really would appreciate it if you would remain during this meeting." The dean sat down and things got more and more interesting.

The chairman started by pointing out that my prospectus was rejected because I apparently lacked sophistication in the matter of sound research methodology suitable at the doctoral dissertation level. I resisted this assumption, of course, and presented my copy of Dr. Jack's letter that indicated otherwise. It was at that point that I learned that the dean of the College of Liberal Arts at the University was not an honorable man. As if pre-planned, he became indignant over the "gall" of Dr. Michael to interfere with the activities of another faculty at a University at which he no longer served. "Dr. Michael is no longer here, Mr. Hoored, and his concerns are of no significance in this matter." As I resisted, the dean then said," I'm tired of listening to your "drivel." I couldn't believe what I was hearing. I actually asked him to repeat the word. "I said *"drivel,* Mr.Hoored." The dean had been pleasant in earlier meetings, but in the meeting with the psychologists he chose to insult me.

As I reflected on that meeting over the years I became more convinced that the dean did that to me for the intended purpose of getting me to explode in anger so that I could be dismissed as arrogant and uncooperative, as had been previously claimed by the chairman. As humiliated as I felt, I actually thanked that group for their time and, like a whipped dog, I headed for home.

The psychology department chairman then made a mistake. In order to reinforce the position that the psychologists had taken in the meeting, he wrote that same dean a letter supposedly recanting the discussion that had taken place. He sent me a copy. The letter was grossly inaccurate, misleading and self-serving. I was so enraged by it that I spent the next two days on my little *Smith Carona* writing out what *really* happened during that meeting, noting that I was never given the opportunity to challenge the validity of the criticisms that resulted in my prospectus rejection. No consideration had been given to the professional opinion of Dr. Michael, who served on the editorial board of the leading science journal on operant conditioning and who supported the acceptability of my rejected dissertation prospectus.

Nearly setting my little typewriter afire turned out to be a bold move on my part as I sent a copy of my letter and that of Dr. Michael's and other related letters up the chain of command (remember?) to the dean of the graduate division of the University! One week later, I called that dean's office for an appointment. I am not a man of courage, but it was becoming more and more evident that I was being victimized and I knew I had it all in writing. What to do? What *can* I do? Should I just quit? What about my twenty-year dream of being a doctor of psychology? Now tell me, my good reader, what would *you* have done?

The dean of the graduate school was an understanding, sincere fellow, who took the time to hear me out. He was much like the dean of the College of Liberal Arts was at first, before his real colors were revealed. He listened to me for about an hour. A week later he sent me a thoughtful letter in which he encouraged me to begin my additional course work and take the repeated comprehensive exam and then to finish my dissertation. In other words, he was saying that I must follow the dictates of the psychology chairman. He could see how unfair the requirements were, but still he would not help me.

I took my case even higher. to the vice-president of the state University! In his final statement, he agreed with the graduate dean and the Liberal Arts College dean that it was up to the department chairman to determine what would be required of me to complete my program. I was defeated. There was nothing I could do. I knew that even if I followed his recommendations, however unfair, I would eventually be failed, just as my prospectus had failed. He had said on the first day that we met, "You'll get no help from me." He meant it and I knew he would never let me get my degree.

I finally decided that I had to give up. It didn't matter how much I wanted to get my degree. It didn't matter how unjust the requirements were. It didn't matter how much I had been wronged. It didn't matter that I had letters that proved that my prospectus had been unfairly and brutally rejected. It didn't matter that I was being canceled out of the program. Nothing was to matter, the psychology department chairman had the backing of the University administrators all the way up the line and I was screwed.

You know, in a situation like that you have to find some way to console yourself. So I began to think more of the good job I had at Phoenix Community College, the wonderful wife who supported my efforts through the years and those beautiful kids who loved their daddy even if he was absent for so many of their early years, lost in his own selfish dream - a dream that was not to be fulfilled. "After all," I asked myself, "was it really *that* important?" With all of the good things in my life, did I *really* need to have a Ph.D? I decided that very few people get everything they want in life and that I had what was most important. I reluctantly admitted to myself that I had wasted several years fighting with those at the University and that my family had paid more than enough. And so, I gave up.

But it continued to nag at me. I brooded as the months went by. I couldn't accept what happened to me. I would teach my classes and then go back to my office and stare at the wall. It was so unfair. It was so cruel. It was so costly to my career. It was... well, what could I say? It was just "drivel," remember?

How I hated that word!

CHAPTER SEVEN

EVERYTHING CHANGED

Then, one afternoon, everything changed! Yes, everything actually changed! There was nothing special about that afternoon. It was the same as any other, just another depressing, self-pitying session that served no purpose whatever. Brooding as usual, I was almost startled when for some unknown reason a brand new idea hit me. "Don," I told myself, "You have been presenting your frustrating case to the *wrong* people." I was almost immediately filled with a sense of renewed resolve. Immediately, I knew what I had to do.

I slammed my briefcase, closing it on two years worth of disappointment and anger in the form of a dozen or so letters and notes, tossed it into the back seat of my Volkswagen bug and headed for the University. Once on campus, I hunted down the College of Law! No appointment, no announcement, no preparation, with no pre planning, I walked in cold and requested an opportunity to tell my story to any attorney who was interested in faculty-student conflicts at the graduate level!

That was the afternoon when I first met John Morris LLD, a tall black man with "peeper" glasses on the end of his nose who just happened to be a doctor of laws. "Come in and let's chat," he said. And chat we did, for nearly two hours. I could detect right away that he was not a man who would tolerate any blather (drivel?) from anyone. I began by telling him about my personal history, from the military service as a draftee from Arizona through my three degrees, my successful presentation of my master's thesis before the first graduate student symposium in the psychology department, my three years of lecturing experience at that very University and my subsequent teaching as a professor at Phoenix College. All of this, before I began to tell him the reason for my arrival that afternoon at the College of Law.

I was caught, I told him, between my intense desire to complete my program on the one hand and my personal, desperate fear of fighting on against the odds when I was convinced that I had been wrongfully treated by all at the various levels of the University administration. "I can't let go of this," I pleaded. "I can't handle the humiliation, the insulting conflict, the unbearable stress that the psychology department chairman was subjecting me to with the cruel support of the deans. Near tears, I then told him of the reason for my arrival at the College of Law.

Dr. Morris listened to me as no other had before him. He read letter after letter as I handed them to him in the order of their occurrence. I could feel his developing interest. I could feel him occasionally pausing to study me. I could feel something happening. I didn't know what, but this time it was different. Suddenly, Dr. Morris spun around in his chair, reached for the telephone and told the operator that he wanted to speak with the dean of the College of Liberal Arts "Hey, George," he said. "This is Morris over in the college of law. What in Hell has been happening over the last couple of years to doctoral candidate Donald Huard in your psychology department?"

Sitting there, I felt my entire nervous system go into an uncontrollable panic. It was like what happened when there was suddenly what we called "incoming" in the military, meaning the arrival of mortar or artillery fire. You better get your ass in a hole somewhere in a hurry if you want to survive. I wanted to hide beneath the doctor's desk. The conversation with the dean lasted for about fifteen minutes, after which Dr. Morris chased me out of his office with an extended hand and a promise that he would look more seriously into my case and further advise me. "Let me make copies of those letters before you go," he suggested. Curiously, I never saw or heard from this man again. No phone call. No letter. No nothing. Still, I will be forever indebted to him for what followed.

About two weeks later, I was on the stairs in the psychology building for some unrelated reason that I can't remember when all of a sudden I ran into none other than the dean who had grown so tired of my "drivel" in that humiliating meeting with the psychologists. "Oh, Hi, Mr. Hooored," he said. "I was just going to call you to give you some good news. I want you to see the new department chairman as soon as you can. He may be able to arrange for the setting up of a new committee and the completion of your program."

I wasted no time. I had not met this new professor, but was in his office in a matter of minutes. Within a very short time, I realized that this clinical psychologist was expecting me and that he had been aggressively prepped for the occasion by the former chairman. I was in for further humiliation, this time by a real pro. "Don, you have offended a number of people in this department and you should consider it a gift that anyone would be willing to serve on a committee for you." The first chairman had primed him very well. I humbled myself. "I feel bad about the problems I have had in the department." Immediately, he responded, "Oh, we have no problem with you, Don, you are the one with the problem." "But I ...," I began. He put his hand up near my face and cut me off with, "Oh, don't try to defend yourself, Don, you are in a position of no strength whatever."

It was obvious that this new chairman was enjoying putting the arrogant candidate (ask chairman number one) in his proper place. "If you think that you will ever get your degree out of this department you will have to place yourself in the *position of a beggar*. Then, you *might* be given a chance to complete your dissertation."

49

Again, fully two years after the first time, I was feeling almost uncontrollable rage. I wanted to climb over the top of that man's desk and smash his grille, but instead, I had to try to convince him that I would be willing to do whatever would be required to get my degree. Even crawl. I felt the knife being twisted in my gut and I couldn't even scream. Having humiliated me until he was thoroughly satisfied, the new chairman suggested that I confer with a new man in the department who just *might* be willing to help me. "See Dr. Heygood. He might be willing to talk to you..."

After calming down for a few days and reliving that terrible experience, I began to take note of the fact that Dr. "Austin" had not mentioned the continuing requirement for me to take any additional course work, let alone any need to retake a repeat comprehensive examination. There was no mention in this meeting of the unreasonable demands of Dr. Gus in my meeting with the first chairman. I wondered why? Then it hit me! John Morris LLD had apparently convinced them that they would be wise to encourage completion of my program. I may be wrong, but it is quite possible that this attorney may have convinced the dean that if I were to seek legal retribution with the documentation that I had in writing, it could turn into a case somewhat embarrassing to the University.

So, as instructed, I met with Dr. Robert E. Heygood. He was an entirely different kind of psychology professor. He was in his mid fifties, a specialist in experimental method and data analysis. More importantly, he was friendly, easy going and nonthreatening to talk to, a man with quiet confidence and a sincere desire to be helpful to any student who showed potential. Dr. "Bob" wouldn't let me tell him about all of the troubles I had with two other members of the department over the years. "Let's just look ahead, Don, and we will design a good research project for you, one that will result in the successful completion of your program." That's what we did and it worked as he said it would.

Can you imagine what the supportive attitude of this man meant to me as one who had a history of disappointment and despair, who desperately tried for several years to survive the vindictive pressures applied by two unprofessional men who conspired to prevent my success? There are no sufficient words available to me that can adequately express my sense of appreciation for the efforts of the attorney John Morris, my former professor Jack Michael from the University of Western Michigan who wrote that supportive letter on my behalf that challenged the arbitrary rejection of my prospectus and Dr. Heygood who with his positive attitude and sincere style enabled me to get my degree!

I remember the many hours we spent in Dr. Bob's office, one-on-one in front of the wall that was almost all blackboard. He chaulked out the steps, taught me some good design methods and statistical techniques that became so handy in my own teaching in subsequent years. He signed my petition to the graduate college for some additional time to complete my work. It was approved. He helped me recruit four additional professors who were willing to serve on my new committee. We held "data" meetings in which the full committee would review my progress and make constructive suggestions. At last, I was seeing a degree of cooperation by faculty members dedicated to my progress rather than motivated for mean spirited obstruction intended to thwart the fulfillment of my personal dream. Can you imagine what that meant to me?

A sad, but interesting side note: Several months into the process my father passed away. It was a most difficult time for my family. A data meeting had been scheduled for the morning of the funeral. Dr. Heygood explained the situation to the committee members and they proceeded in my absence, further advancing the development of my dissertation. Gradually I began to realize that my committee chairman was "tuning" my head in those one-on-one meetings in his office. He was tuning me in preparation for the day when I would be standing in defense of my dissertation before a larger committee, thereby completing all requirements for the Ph.D. degree. "If they ask you why you used this design, then answer in this way..." he suggested. "If they want to know why you used the analysis of variance statistical technique and the Duncan Multiple Range Test, tell them this..." He was tuning my head, slowly building in a little confidence, getting me ready for that Thursday afternoon in August of 1971 when, after two and a half hours of dissertation defense, **Dr. Huard** was congratulated by all present.

As soon as I got my degree, my salary at Phoenix College was increased by about $6,000 per year. As you can see, that amounted to a lot of money when considered over the next thirty-five years of my career. I didn't persist for the money however, I suffered through the program because I wanted something that badly, because I knew that I had been treated wrongly and I wanted it made right. I could not have done this by myself. In the end, I finally got the help I needed. I have learned that a truly self-made man is very rare, indeed. It takes a lot of determination to get where you want to go, but it also takes the recruitment of some others who believe in you. And a bit of luck, though in my case, that luck was a long time coming.

It took the willing cooperation of a lot of professors to get me through that program. I had to regain confidence in some new faculty members after a painful history of so much disappointment. I had to overcome that sad history and restore my own confidence. I had to believe in *me*.

CHAPTER EIGHT

REVENGE - A MEAL BEST SERVED COLD

Fully five years after that terrible, frustrating experience at the University during which I was insulted, degraded, belittled and made to feel nearly unbearable anxiety and trepidation at the hands of two vicious professors of psychology, I received a letter from the dean of the University graduate college. I was amazed that I would be asked to provide an honest evaluation of my doctorate training program at the University. Needless to say, I was absolutely delighted to comply.

"Dear Dr. Sanders," I began. "Thank you for your letter expressing an interest in an evaluation of my doctorate program at the state University in the department of psychology. Be assured that I would not have been inclined to provide you with the following information without your request that I do so."

I then proceeded to lay out in considerable detail the treatment I had been subjected to by the acting chairman of the psychology department, then by the following chairman and by the dean of the College of Liberal Arts as I struggled to get my dissertation completed. I stressed the arbitrary way that I was humiliated at each step of the way by Drs. "Gus," "Austin" and dean "George," out of sheer vindictiveness for a period of nearly two years. My letter, accompanied by several other letters was presented to illustrate my disdain. It was three pages long!

What an absolute joy it was, to be given such a great opportunity!

What a great feeling it was, that of delivering a most delicious meal, a meal best served cold! During our first meeting when I requested the establishment of a committee to help me develop a dissertation, Dr. Gus told me that I would not get any help from him. I relayed in my letter that Dr. Austin said that I would have to put myself in the *position of a beggar* if I were to get through the program. Dean George accused me of talking *drivel,* as the three men undercut my efforts to set up the needed committee to be involved in my training.

I had the letters. I had the signatures. I had the evidence.

I detailed my story as it evolved over a two year period. I noted the unreasonable demands that were arbitrarily placed on me by the chairman for additional course work, a repeat of my successful comprehensive examination and a dissertation prospectus that would be reviewed by him and two of his own associates. The reasons for the prospectus rejection were noted in my letter as well as a copy of the challenge of those reasons by a board member of the leading science journal of operant conditioning who wrote in support of the intent of my prospective research. In his view, the prospectus had merit, yet it was rejected by the chairman who was not aware of current research.

Dr. Jack Michael, the board member of the *Journal of Experimental Analysis of Behavior* wrote, "Of the three major criticisms of Mr. Huard's prospectus that were used as a basis for rejection, two were unwarranted in light of recent research techniques and the third criticism posed only a minor problem that could be corrected with ease. I conclude that Mr. Huard's proposal *had* merit." Yet, it *was* rejected.

I detailed the eventual support I got from Dr. Morris of the College of Law and, mostly to my own personal satisfaction, I gave the full names of the people involved. One thing I do regret to this day fifty years later is that I decided not to send copies of the letters directly to the mean men involved. I should have requested that copies of the letters be placed in the personnel files of each man.

I have asked myself over and over why I was singled out by Dr.

Gus to have my successful completion of all of the requirements for the degree including the final comprehensive examination found inadequate by the more current standards (as determined by him) in such a manner as to prevent me from setting up a committee to finish my program.

Did I deserve to have my footing tripped only a few yards from the finish line of a marathon that took years to run? Why? Why did Gus say, "You'll get no help from me?" Why did he go out of his way to stop my progress? Why did he set up the unreasonable additional requirements other than out of his personal animus toward me? When he did so and when I complained about it to the dean of the college as I was told to do so by another faculty member, he refused to respond to my plea. Saddest of all was the fact that at all subsequent levels of the administration up to and including the office of the vice-president, that spiteful chairman was supported!

Apparently the dean of the College of Liberal Arts did not have the courage to point out the unfairness of the new rules imposed on me in an arbitrary manner by the psychology department chairman. He had to have known that what Dr. Gus had done was wrong! Yet, Dean George decided to support the chairman in a "brutal" way (using the dean's own word) at my expense, calling my protestations "drivel."

The years of frustration to which I was subjected were cruel, unnecessary and the result of unprofessional conduct on the parts of a number of colluding professors, deans and even the vice-president of the University.

The objective became one of protection of the University from the legitimate claims of a qualified, successful doctoral candidate irregardless of the issue of right or wrong. It's amazing that I was able to finish a dissertation and eventually get my Ph.D. degree!

Not wanting to be totally negative as I wrote my three page evaluation letter requested by the dean of the graduate college five years later, I added some comments of appreciation for several other professors who finally treated me with fairness, most notably Dr. Robert Heygood who guided me on my final project and disciplined my brain for my dissertation defense.

Nearly fifty years later and at the age of eighty-six and as a graduate with three degrees from my own state University and nearly three years as a lecturer there, I find myself with conflicted feelings as an alumnus of that institution. In the last forty years I have not returned to the campus because of the treatment I received and the painful memories that a visit would generate.

I was treated shamefully, in an unprofessional manner by two cruel psychologists and a complicit dean of the College of Liberal Arts in what I see today as a conspiracy.

It's sad. It's a very sad story. It never should have happened. Somewhere along the line some one should have called a halt to the unprofessional conduct of those who conspired to prevent the fulfillment of my dream. When it was graduation time for my Ph.D. degree to be conferred, I didn't even attend the ceremony. I had the administration mail me my degree. I have never returned to the campus of Arizona State University. How sad...

CHAPTER NINE

"WELCOME HOME, DR. DADDY"

Excited as I was with my new teaching contract at Phoenix College in 1963, I had to consider the potential consequences of leaving the University a year too soon, thereby losing out on an opportunity to complete my doctoral dissertation with my already established doctoral committee chaired by a very capable professor. I told him about my concern before signing the new contract and was told that it was possible to do a dissertation "on the run."

I didn't know that a year later my mentor would take a new job himself at the University of Hawaii, leaving me with the problem of setting up a new committee. The college catalog permitted completion of a dissertation up to five years beyond the completion of the doctorate comprehensive examinations, which I had successfully passed.

To my complete surprise, I was advised that it would be necessary for me to re-take those exams, then complete a research paper before I would be permitted to do the dissertation. Just three years had gone by since I left the University, so I felt justified in requesting additional time to finish my program without re-examination. My petition was denied! In as much as it takes at least a year to prepare for "comps," I felt that the requirement for re-examination was unfair. Notably with consideration of the fact that I had not left the field and had been teaching during that interim.

I didn't know what to do. At the suggestion of another professor I consulted with the dean of the college of liberal arts about my concern. I had successfully completed my foreign language requirement (French), presented my master's thesis at a symposium before the faculty and fellow graduate students and finished thirty more semester hours of doctorate level coursework. Then, after a year of special study I passed the twelve hour doctorate comprehensive examination that extended over two highly stressful days in 1963.

A little instruction about the nature of a comprehensive examination might be useful at this point. Mine consisted of a two day written exam over four distinct areas of the field of psychology: the history of psychology, the history of the psychology of learning (called conditioning), behavioral modification techniques in the area of clinical psychology and research design and statistics.

After a year of preparation, on Labor Day in 1963 I wrote for seven hours on the first two areas, then six more hours on the next day. My graduate committee passed me on my writing in all of those areas.

By that time I had acquired some teaching experience at that same University, so I used that reference to gain support. I performed as a lecturer in my own classes often taught in a large lecture hall, including several I taught with over 140 students!

Much to my surprise after my many conflicted meetings with resistant faculty members, I had the great good fortune to meet Dr. "Bob," (as I have called him) and with him, I got along beautifully! I learned to respect him immensely, not just for the help he gave me, but also because he was so sincere and considerate. He seemed to be very sure of himself. His cooperative style, more than anything else, is why I managed to get my degree.

The relationship that was eventually established between Dr. Bob and me was incredible! He was a brilliant mentor, a most capable researcher and he was willing to direct my program! He was one who wanted to stress my future as we worked together over the next year. I spent hours in his office week after week while he was instructing me individually, using his blackboard and chalk, writing out potential research designs and suggesting methods of statistical analyses that would be pertinent to my study. Looking back on it now, I realize what a marvelous experience it was for me. I was getting the opportunity to learn from a most competent professor who was truly intent on helping me fulfill my potential. After being treated so badly by others in the psychology department, I was, at last, seeing the best of graduate dissertation preparatory training.

We set up a new committee with the doctor suggesting the other four members who might be interested in my project. We held several project design meetings and input from the others helped to strengthen what had become my dissertation proposal. Finally, I had approval of the design and approval in the graduate college of a petition for an extension of time to complete the study.

Because my new study was in the area of language conditioning, not one for animal research, I had to use an experimental method that involved short-term conditioning of hundreds of psychology students in dozens of "borrowed" classes both at Phoenix College and at the University. That meant getting the cooperation of other teachers, which I was able to do.

I would carry a heavy projector and written instruction sheets, data collection sheets and special pencils to each class to be tested. The thirty minute procedure was cumbersome at first in the "pilot" studies. Then it became refined and appropriate as a good method for "teasing out" the data needed for testing my experimental hypotheses.

I remember a specific day when I raced across the campus carrying a projector and supplies by myself in 110 degree July heat, thinking that I would surely die before the day was over. When I got to the prearranged class, I was so nervous presenting to the students that I could hardly be heard. When it was over, my mentor said, "You have to speak louder, Don." As the time went on, my presentations were clearer and smoother and eventually I had all of the data I needed.

The data analysis committee meetings were quite helpful, teaching me some mathematical techniques that I used later in my own teaching of classes in statistical methods at Phoenix College. Some of those techniques are mentioned in my book *Behavioral Statistics: Methods of Analysis and Persuasion* published by Kendal/Hunt Publishing in 1992.

After months of data compilation and analysis, I was ready for the final write-up of the dissertation and the preparation for its defense before the final examining committee. It was a time that I began to see the special goodness of Dr. Bob. Two occasions stand out in my memory. I had taken the summer off from my teaching at Phoenix College and the final defense was set for August 20, 1971.

One afternoon as I worked feverishly typing my own manuscript (only a foolish candidate does that) in my little cubicle in the department filled with crunched up, throw away copies of many pages filling the room behind me, the Dr. dropped in to see how I was doing. Seeing my tempo and my panic, he paused just long enough to say some magic words to me. "You'll make it, you know," he said, "Stay cool. It's working out fine." He didn't know what those words meant to me at that time, but then, maybe he did...

Another time as I worked on some of the technical graphs needed to illustrate the trends in the data, he came in, studied my progress then left for about an hour or so. When he returned he handed me several graphs that he had drawn. As he handed them to me he said, "Here, use these for pages 137 and 138, they will work out just fine." I was so appreciative of his efforts on my behalf. About half way through the ten month process I became aware of how he was preparing me for the dissertation defense. By the time my defense took place, he had me fine tuned and even confident that I was in for a very special, very big day with the big boys.

Understandably, I couldn't sleep the night before my very special day. The oral dissertation defense was scheduled for two hours at 3 o'clock that Thursday afternoon. Present were my five committee members, another member who was not a committee member and a dean from the graduate college. I had been advised by my professor to present a summary of my research and some conclusions over the first forty-five minutes and then I would be questioned for the remaining time.

The title of my dissertation was *The effects of Stimulus Intensity on the Conditioning of Word Meaning*. Knowing that our "guest" from the graduate college was not familiar with the classical conditioning process basic to my study, I proceeded to teach the Pavlovian conditioning paradigm at a very low level as I had done for my own psychology students at Phoenix College. Then, I planned to proceed to the complexities of my research.

I was suddenly interrupted by a question from one of the members. "What makes it work, Don," he asked? I thought a bit, then answered, "I don't know, sir." Out of the comer of my eye, I saw the graduate dean shift in his chair as his facial muscles tightened. Probably, he was thinking, "Oh, Oh, this fellow is in trouble!"

However, I pointed out that even Ivan Pavlov himself never provided that answer. "Pavlov claimed the association was dependent on irradiation across the higher areas of the cerebral cortex, a process he was never able to demonstrate." I added, "In recent research, attempts have been made to correlate these changes with measured changes in RNA, the biological cousin of the hereditary molecule DNA that is said by some to store memory. However, the correlations have never been established."

A most marvelous thing happened. The questioner was completely satisfied with my answer! He smiled broadly, a smile that I interpreted as something like, "OK, the candidate is not going to try to snow the members of the committee. He's going to admit what he doesn't know, now let's get on with the business of the day."

The business of the day proceeded so smoothly that I could hardly believe it! Soon I was fielding questions just as Dr. Bob had instructed me and it was all working. When I got cornered a little, the professors seemed more amused than concerned. However, at 5:15 P.M. they were still asking me more questions and I began to get a little nervous. "Why are they keeping me so long," I wondered? At 5:40 they had me leave the room. After the longest fifteen minutes in the history of the entire universe, the door opened and one of them reached his hand out to me saying "Let me be the first to congratulate you, **Doctor Huard**." I shook hands with the other members of the committee, then spied my open dissertation on the desk, topped with all of the signatures I needed for completion. I cannot adequately describe the feeling of relief and exhaultation that came over me! Thanks to Dr. Bob and so many others, I had been able to beat the system that had been frustrating me for so many months. I was finally able to work successfully with a group of professors committed to my development - the fulfillment of my dream!

Of course, after niceties with the dean and the others on the committee, the first thing I did was to go into the office to call my Marie. "It's all over, honey. Now we can go on living again." Later, as I walked to my car, feeling a thousand pounds lighter, carrying my precious briefcase as though it contained expensive jewelry, I paused to ask my mentor, "Why did they keep me so long? Don't they have families to go home to," I asked? "They were interested, Don" was the only answer I got. What an answer!

Before leaving the east end of the valley, I had a special place I was compelled to visit, the Green Acres Cemetery where my Dad was buried. There I sobbed out a few years' worth of tension as I shared my success with my father, wishing that he could know how much I missed him and how much I wanted him to be proud of my accomplishment. I could hear my sister Shirley telling me, "He knows, Don. He knows."

Stopping by in Scottsdale to give Mom the news, I came upon a delightful surprise. It seemed warm in the house. Then I realized that my mother had been burning candles in every room in the house! Her whole afternoon had been spent praying that all of those people at the University would be good to her son Donnie. Moms are like that, you know. God bless you, Mom, I miss you so much.

The best came last that day. I was exhausted after the stressful examination and during the long drive to our home on the west side of Phoenix. I was afraid that I might fall asleep at the wheel as I drove. I turned off of Camelback road and into our darkened neighborhood, then turned again onto Elm street and finally drove up onto our driveway. As I drove into the carport, the lights of my car illuminated a large colorful sign taped to the front of the utility room. It read:

Welcome home, Doctor Daddy!

"Welcome home, Doctor Daddy!"

AFTERTHOUGHT

Approximately six months after my release from the military in 1954, I began my college studies that were eventually completed with my doctorate in 1971. That's a span of seventeen years. I was then forty-one years old. Not being considered as a "brilliant" student, my first years were somewhat remedial in nature. But as the years went by, I became determined to continue to advance in the world of academia.

I learned many things in addition to the formal training I needed for my profession. Among them is the fact that persistent determination can result in much achievement in the long run. I learned that wanting something bad enough to go after it with one's heart and soul is a positive thing. Refusal to give up on a dream can pay off in time.

I learned that you don't go to college to "get" a degree. Instead, you must earn it. You have to build it. It takes a very long time and requires a great amount of self-discipline. The higher you go in academia, the greater the challenge to achieve. Therefore, we feel a greater sense of accomplishment after each successful step along the way. I learned that there is no such thing as a self-made man or woman. Anyone who accomplishes much, owes much to those who helped along the way. No one does it alone.

I learned that there are lots of ways to live a productive life. Early adulthood is a time for investigating options, for finding where we best fit. For most of us, it does not involve any higher education. Society needs plumbers, cooks, landscapers, secretaries, machinists, store cashiers and those who stock the shelves, as well as engineers, doctors, lawyers and executives.

The trick is to find where we will best fit in and can be happiest as a person who contributes his or her skills and motivations to making the world a better place. For me, it was in the field of education. I decided to be a teacher. I began my teaching at the University as a psychology lecturer at the age of twenty-eight, just after I was awarded my master's degree. After three years I was hired to teach as a professor at Phoenix College, where I remained for the next thirty-eight years.

After my retirement, I was given the Faculty Emeritus Award in the Maricopa County Community College District. Not bad- for a 115 lb. kid from the desert who became a qualified military infantryman, a veteran and a college professor. It was worth the effort! I had to believe in *me*.

Faculty Emeritus

Awarded To

Dr. Donald Huard

November 25, 2003

In recognition and appreciation
for your service to the
Maricopa County Community College District

_____
GOVERNING BOARD PRESIDENT

_____
CHANCELLOR

ADDENDUM:

LETTERS

This letter sent to Mr. Huard by the University psychology department chairman rejects the candidate's research prospectus.

August 14, 1969
Mr. Donald V. Huard

Dear Mr. Huard

I am sorry to say that your thesis prospectus was unanimously considered unacceptable, in three independent evaluations of it.

The basic problem that you appear to be attempting to examine is whether or not there is a U-shaped relation for a discrimination learning function, with increasing food deprivation levels. Further, you wish to know whether this curve shape, or its parameters, are different at different levels of difficulty in the discrimination task. This latter question would appear to be what you mean by "an interaction effect."

Unfortunately, your design does not permit an examination of either the basic curve issue, or the interaction effect. For example, for a curvilinear relation, you need to have three points, at the minimum. That is, to represent a U function there must be some relatively low level of deprivation, some moderate level of deprivation and then a relatively high level of deprivation to complete the U in the learning curve of error rate. With your design, you could not find a U-shaped curve if there was one and the question could not be answered. It is hard to conceive of your being interested in this issue and not realizing this elementary fact.

We turn now from your deprivation conditions to your discrimination task. Your so-called difficult discrimination task is actually impossible for most of its phases. Since there is no exteroceptive stimulus, the only factor that can be discriminated is the time during which no reinforcement was obtainable (which is as you wished it). but the time duration of S+ and S- conditions in this mixed schedule will, for the most part, be the same.

Thus, we find that both deprivation and discrimination were treated in a way that precluded your examining the issues that you posed.

We now come to your attempt to be careful in design (I suppose), and run a reverse condition, where the animals on one deprivation level were switched to the other (for both deprivation groups). But, instead of trying them in a new discrimination task, you have them merely performing on an already learned task. Clearly this would not be a learning curve function anymore, but some sort of function on disturbances caused by changing amounts of feeding. You could run them on the same task, in a reverse learning situation. But, this would require running them to a criterion of performance, rather than some arbitrary number of days.

This last section, then, is just some more bad experimental design. This prospectus is indicative of a need for far more sophistication. Assuming adequate potential, that means more education.

I suggest that you come in and talk to me.

Sincerely,
Associate Professor
Acting Chairman, Psychology

This letter was sent to the Dean of the University College of Liberal Arts as a response to the rejection letter written by the acting chairman of the University psychology department. Written by an Associate editor of the science journal *The Journal of the Experimental Analysis of Behavior*, it challenges the basis for the chairman's rejection of the candidate's prospectus.

Oct 3, 1969
George A. Peek Jr. Dean
College of Liberal Arts

Dear Dr. Peek,

At the request of Donald V. Huard, whom I knew as a graduate student when I was a faculty member in the Psychology Department at A.S.U, I am sending my reaction to his dissertation prospectus, and to Dr. Levine's reaction to the prospectus.

As prospectuses go, this is not bad. Dr. Levine's first comment is basically irrelevant. Mr. Huard does not propose to demonstrate a U-shaped curve, but only to analyze discrimination ratios and interresponse-time distributions at high and low deprivations for tasks of high and low difficulty. It is historically true that people have been interested in the U-shaped characteristic of this function, but it is clear from Mr. Huard's initial statement that this is not his major interest.

The second comment by Dr. Levine is quite relevant, however, the discrimination condition that he calls difficult seems an essentially unsatisfactory one. On the other hand, it would seem so easy to salvage that condition and my first reaction to the prospectus, had it been submitted to me for evaluation, would have been to suggest to Mr. Huard that he alter his difficult discrimination condition somewhat. With that change, his dissertation has a certain merit.

However, this seems to be somewhat irrelevant in view of the present setting. It appears to me that the dissertation prospectus is being used as a test of some sort to determine whether Mr. Huard should be permitted to work on a dissertation or not without taking further coursework. This seems quite unusual to me, but of course, there are no rules forbidding such an arrangement.

I have been directing doctoral dissertations since 1956 and have had many submitted to me that were in worse shape than Mr. Huard's. They constituted the basis for a rather complete instructional relationship between me and the doctoral candidate.

This type of relationship clearly isn't Dr. Levine's aim in this situation, and I have no experience to draw upon with respect to the use of a dissertation prospectus as a test. Had I been Dr. Levine, I think I would have turned the prospectus over to one of the younger members of the department who is more familiar with this area of work and ask him if he would be willing to function as a dissertation chairman for the research. That person could then have interacted with Mr. Huard and if in fact Mr. Huard had been unable to ultimately arrive at a satisfactory prospectus, after his initial efforts had been criticized, then perhaps he could be required to take further work.

All of this may seem like meddling in the affairs of another department. For this I apologize. My motivation is simply to correct what I think is a misleading impression of Mr. Huard. Dr. Levine's letter would make him appear to be an unusually incompetent doctoral candidate. I do not believe this to be the case. I knew Mr. Huard when he was a graduate student and he was a very capable graduate student. It is true that he has been working as a teacher in the field for several years and during this period he was not really functioning as a graduate student. As a result, some of his graduate student behavior may seem a bit unpolished. But, in spite of this, his prospectus, considered within the framework of the operant conditioning literature of which Dr. Levine may be unaware, seems worth further development to me.

Sincerely,

Jack Michael, Ph.D.
Associate Editor of
The Journal of the Experimental Analysis
of Behavior
University of Western
Michigan

Books by Donald V. Huard, Ph.D.

Emeritus professor of
Psychology Phoenix
Community College

Behavioral Statistics: An introduction to the
basic methods of analysis and persuasion. 1992 *

You Need a Red Hat	2002
Youth Deficit Disorder	2004
The Violence that Prevails	2007
Teenagers: What will cigarettes, Booze, 'Safe' Sex and drugs do for you?	2012
Where Grandpa's Been... An Autobiography	2015 *

* Publications placed in the Library of Congress of the United States of America in Washington, D. C.

ABOUT THE AUTHOR

Most survival stories involve threat of physical trauma or escape from actual physical harm. Examples included in this book were experienced by the author as a young soldier at the time of America's involvement in the Korean conflict in the early 1950s. Merely surviving sixteen weeks of military basic training as a 115 lb. draftee "momma's boy" was challenging enough. But, I did survive. On one occasion. I was involved in the crashing of a light military aircraft that nearly took my life and the life of my pilot. We crashed off of the end of a runway down into a deep ravine, completely destroying a military version of a Cessna 180 plane being used to supply engineering surveyors in the Alaska wilderness.

I recall being thrown out of the plane and being tossed deeper into the ravine. There I was, alive, but looking up at the plane's left wing dangling from its body, hanging by only a wire used to control one of its flaps. The landing gear was badly sprung out of shape, a tire had exploded, the propeller was broken and the plane's body was a mess. But, neither of us was seriously injured. That day, survival was the name of the game.

A second time, while I was still in the military, I survived a serious threat to the loss of flight of my DeHaveland Beaver, a six passenger, radial engine-powered plane that suddenly lost power and was likely to crash into the mountain terrain. Almost miraculously, an applied restart procedure worked. I. and four other passengers survived.

Years later, as a Ph.D. candidate for a doctorate degree at Arizona State University my character and educational competence were challenged in a manner that threatened my likely success in the program. Fifteen years of course work. Examinations and laboratory training in the field of experimental psychology were deemed insufficient to meet the extended requirements conferred on me. I met radical requirements imposed unfairly by several mean-spirited senior professors who became intent on preventing the successful completion of my dissertation.

For three years. I fought the added requirements by appealing up the chain of command all the way to the vice-president of the University. I was finally allowed to complete my work after recruiting the help of an attorney in the College of Law. Again, survival became the name of the game.

But, the greatest threats to survival in my life were yet to come. On two very sad occasions, I was faced with devastating loss, the deaths of two wives, the first, of Marie at the age of just forty-nine. She was the mother of our four children, Christopher (20), Theresa (19) and our twin sons David and Gregory. The twins were fourteen at the time of their mother's death. A strong loving marriage of twenty-three years ended when I had just turned fifty.

The loss of a loved one, a spouse or child has a profound effect on the emotional lives of its survivors. I was devastated by the loss of my first wife. Writing about the feelings of grief that I experienced a few days after the funeral will indicate the depth of my pain. I sobbed uncontrollably one day over the loss of Marie, telling my oldest son that I felt that I had lost everything in the world that was important to me. Chris immediately responded to what I said, "But Dad," he said. "You still have *US!*" His comment forced me into the realization that the grief was not exclusively mine, that our children were also suffering the loss of Mom and I needed to be strong for them in the critical time of their need. As well as my own.

Several months following Marie's death, my younger brother

advised me of my need to reach out to others similarly stricken with painful loss of a spouse. His suggestion resulted in my first attendance at a meeting of a social group called *Parents Without Partners* frequented by folks who were alone with parental responsibilities. The first meetings were frightening for me. I felt out of place, the return home after each meeting left me feeling empty, isolated and alone.

One evening I began to notice a lovely middle-aged lady who was welcoming new attendees to the group. She seemed especially friendly and even agreed to risk injury from my unskilled version of the two-step. From the beginning I enjoyed being with her. Though it was a matter of only six months or so since I suffered the terrible loss of Marie, I was attracted to the exceptionally friendly personality of the new lady I met at the parents without partners meeting. She was in her mid-forties, a woman who had raised her own three children in a marriage that ended in divorce ten or so years before we met. Dancing with her at the meetings led to an occasional dinner date that led to a new developing relationship that enriched my life for the next forty years!

Margie and I married less than a year later, agreeing to join our two families into one with a new Dad and Mom and seven near adult children. It was a tumultuous marriage at times, with lots of child stepparent conflicts that could never have been predicted. But together Margie and I made our marriage work. Over the years, we grew as close as a couple ever could, well into our declining years. Ours was a marriage of oldsters fully devoted to each other to the very end. Then I found myself once again facing a devastating loss. My Margie passed away at the age of eighty-five, just after I turned ninety years of age.

Surviving that loss has become the most severe challenge of my long life. I have learned that the more devoted one becomes to a marriage partner, the more difficult it is to adjust to the loss of that love.

I am left with overwhelming emptiness, the hollowest feelings of personal loneliness. And again, the need to survive. Alone again, it seems as though there is no escape from the emotional pain of my loss. Her incredibly natural friendliness won me over in a relationship that should have lasted forever. Anyone who came to know Margie came to love her. Family and dozens of friends were offered her grandmotherly advice whether or not they asked for it. We were the loving grandparents and great grandparents of forty-eight children! So many of her friends and grand children have found support in her loving counsel.

I have known true loves in my long life that I will never forget. Each will last forever while I do my best to give my existence new meaning. In each case, I lost a precious treasure of love. In each case, I have had to rebuild my life purpose. The French phrase *Raison de Est* seems to describe the death of one's spouse as the loss of a *reason for being*. The mere passage of time will ease the sadness and slowly replace it with fond memories as I search for that new meaning in my life. Even at the age of ninety, I must continue to believe in *me*...

Printed in the United States
by Baker & Taylor Publisher Services